Macmillan Studies in Religion

# The gospel in the making

A study of Mark, Matthew and Luke

Macmillan Studies in Religion
*Series editor: W.N. Greenwood*

# The gospel in the making

## A study of Mark, Matthew and Luke

*Ruth T. Duckworth*

**MACMILLAN
EDUCATION**

First published 1986
Reprinted 1987

Published by
MACMILLAN EDUCATION LTD
Houndmills, Basingstoke, Hampshire RG21 2XS
and London
Companies and representatives
throughout the world

Designed by Robert Wheeler
Printed in Hong Kong

British Library Cataloguing in Publication Data
Duckworth, Ruth
The Gospel in the making. — Macmillan studies in religion
1. Bible. N.T. Gospels
I. Title  II. Series
226'.0    BS2556
ISBN 0-333-37643-9

# Contents

# Acknowledgements

The author and publishers wish to thank the following who have kindly given permission for the use of copyright material:

Oxford University Press for quotations from Tacitus from *Bettenson: Documents of the Christian Church* (2nd ed. 1963) and from Alan Dale: *The New World* (1967) and *The Winding Quest* (1972)

Viking Penguin Inc for a quotation from *A Passover Haggadah* edited by H Bronstein (1974), illustrated by Leonard Baskin. Copyright © 1974, 1975, 1982 by the Central Conference of American Rabbis. Reprinted by permission of Viking Penguin Inc.

The author and publishers wish to acknowledge the following photograph sources:

Associated Press   pp. 37, 46
British Red Cross Society   pp. 39, 55
British Tourist Association   p. 2
Sister Joan Brown   p. 117
Camera Press   pp. 33, 65, 101, 109
J. Allan Cash   pp. 29, 74, 82
Ron Chapman   pp. 67, 158
Mike Goldwater/Network   p. 143
The Guardian   pp. 68, 105
John and Penny Hubley   p. 47
Imperial War Museum   p. 24 (L)
Kingsway Public Relations   p. 52
Rev Martin Knobs   p. 153
Sheelah Latham   p. 72
City Art Gallery Manchester   p. 16 (L)
Mansell   pp. 11, 16 (R)
R Manson   p. 88
National Maritime Museum   p. 45
Popperfoto   pp. 24 (R), 79, 97
Save the Children Fund   p. 125
Tony Stone Worldwide   p. 25
The Tate Gallery   p. 128
John Topham Picture Library   pp. 90, 138
USPG   p. 18
World Bank   p. 43
World Council of Churches   p. 16 (B)
Zefa Picture Library (UK) Ltd   p. 53

The publishers have made every effort to trace the copyright holders, but where they have failed to do so they will be pleased to make the necessary arrangements at the first opportunity.

Cover photo:   By kind permission of the Trustees of Sir Stanley Spencer Will Trust/Yale University.

# Preface

Religious Education has undergone profound changes in the recent past. This series, *Macmillan Studies in Religion*, has been planned to take account of these changes with reference to both syllabus content and to those skills of learning which are now required of the student. While each book is independent of others in the series, the general approach adopted by the authors is similar. Each writer has in mind the student who is preparing for entry to public examinations in Religious Studies at 16+ and provision is made for students of a wide range of ability.

Each book, therefore, contains basic factual information together with 'extension material' which gives scope for work at a deeper level and/or further factual material for those who work more quickly. The text also incorporates 'stimulus material' to promote discussion and to foster the skills of understanding and evaluation; these skills are then applied by the student to written work in response to questions.

The approach which is characteristic of this series is one which is objective, fair and balanced. The reader is encouraged to consider a number of differing approaches to the subject matter and to respond to 'the challenging and varied nature of religion' (cf. Aim 2 of the *National Criteria for Religious Studies*, 1985). The first books to be published will bring new perspectives to bear on 'traditional' areas (the Synoptic Gospels and Social and Moral Issues) and to an area which features prominently in all recent syllabuses for 16+ examinations: 'Christianity'.

W.N. Greenwood
*Series editor*

# Introduction

No books have been more carefully studied through the centuries than the Christian gospels. Many great scholars have spent a lifetime examining them. During the last hundred years, especially, a great deal has been learned about them – about the kind of literature they are, about how, when and where they were written, and about what particular passages meant to the people for whom they were originally written.

This book aims at putting some of this scholarship at your disposal, so that you can better understand what you read.

There are four *gospels* in the New Testament. This book studies three of them – the gospels of Mark, Matthew and Luke. People sometimes try to merge these three gospels together so as to make a continuous story of the *life and teaching of Jesus Christ*. In this book, however, the gospels are taken one by one, beginning with the gospel according to Mark, because his is the gospel generally thought to have been written first. (The argument for this is given on pp. 103–4.) Then the gospels of Matthew and of Luke are considered in their turn.

You will find two different kinds of boxes in the text of this book:

First, there are tinted boxes. These contain things for you to do, discuss or think about. Sometimes they are planned to help you study towards an examination. At other times they have nothing to do with examinations, but much to do with life. These are included because we are people, not just passers-of-examinations.

Secondly, there are boxes with rounded corners. These contain more difficult material, which is not essential for you. It is included because it is interesting. But you can take it or leave it according to your time and inclination.

This book has been planned with school examinations in mind. But it also aims at enabling you to appreciate more fully what the gospels have meant to Christians throughout the ages. And also (if you wish), to decide for yourself whether they mean anything important to *you*.

Should your school do anything for you other than help you to pass examinations? If so, what?

# 1 What is a gospel?

A car bomb shatters a police station in Northern Ireland ... a plane is hijacked in the Near East ... an inner-city youth club goes up in flames .... If no group claims responsibility, the question *Who was behind it*? becomes an urgent one. Was it the group that has an obvious motive, or was it a frame-up? Rumours spread: there is suspicion and counter-suspicion, accusation and counter-accusation. Even a long inquiry can fail to clear up the situation to everyone's satisfaction.

Over 1900 years ago, in AD 64, a large part of the city of Rome was in flames. No one knew for certain who had started the fire; but in the marketplaces and in the courts the rumour was spreading that it had been started deliberately on the order of the Emperor Nero himself. Nero had plans for a great building project in Rome, and the fire was conveniently clearing a slum area which would otherwise have had to be demolished. Nero's reputation was such that the rumour was not difficult to believe. He had caused his own mother to be brutally murdered, and had his wife banished and then beheaded. Presumably he would not stop at the destruction of lives and property to further his plans. So the rumour gathered strength.

Nero heard the rumour and was afraid. The Roman historian Tacitus, writing in AD 125, tells us what happened next:

> And so, to get rid of this rumour, Nero set up as the culprits and punished with the utmost refinement of cruelty a class hated for their abominations, who are commonly called Christians. Christus, from whom their name is derived, was executed at the hands of the procurator Pontius Pilate in the reign of Tiberius. Checked for the moment, this superstition broke out again, not only in Judaea, but even in Rome .... Accordingly, arrest was first made of those who confessed to being Christians; then, on their evidence an immense multitude was convicted, not so much because of the charge of arson as because of hatred of the human race. Besides being put to death they were made to serve as objects of amusement; they were dressed in the hides of beasts and torn to death by dogs; others were crucified, others set on fire to serve to light up the night when daylight failed. Nero had thrown open his grounds for the display.
>
> (Tacitus: *Annals* xv, 44; from Bettenson, *Documents of the Christian Church*, OUP, 1953)

*Nero*

This passage is one of the earliest independent proofs we have (independent, that is, of the Christians themselves) of the existence of a Christian community in Rome as early as AD 64. It also gives us some idea of how an intelligent Roman could think of the Christians at that time.

What of the Christians themselves? Would they accept the charges of *superstition*, of *hatred of the human race*? How did they see themselves? What picture would they give of their beliefs, of the way they tried to live?

Here are some extracts from their own writings. Most of them are taken from the Acts of the Apostles, or *What the Apostles Did*, a book written about fifty-five years before Tacitus's history. The extracts from Paul are slightly earlier, written during the reign of Nero. The last was written by Paul when he was actually in prison in Rome, probably during the Nero persecution. (NB The first three quotations are taken from a modern arrangement of the New Testament by Alan Dale, called *The New World*. The last three are from the Revised Standard Version of the Bible, which is the one quoted from throughout this book unless there is a note to the contrary.)

Here then are some of the things the Christians said about themselves, their beliefs and their way of life:

You yourselves (they were speaking to the Jews in Jerusalem) know all about Jesus of Nazareth. He lived and worked among you. All he did was proof enough that God sent him and God was with him. He cured sick people, that was a sign of God's power. You handed him over to the Romans and killed him. This indeed was part of God's plan, for God raised him to life again, death could not be the end of his work . . . God has made the man you killed Leader and Lord . . . (from Acts 2: 22–4, 32)

The Council fetched the friends of Jesus back into the court and had them flogged. They ordered them to stop talking about Jesus, and then set them free again. The friends of Jesus left the court happy men, happy because it was for telling the story of Jesus that they had been treated so shamefully. But they didn't stop telling the people about him, either in the Temple or at home . . . 'The story we are telling you', they said, 'is the plain truth. We are only talking about what we have seen for ourselves. God's power in us is proof of it too, the power he gives to all who obey him.' (from Acts, chapter 5)

They (those who believed) lived together and shared everything with one another. They sold their property and possessions and shared the money out so that nobody went without anything he needed. Every day they went to the Temple to worship, and met at home to *break the loaf* together. They shared their meals together with real happiness. All this was their way of thanking God for all he had done for them. The people in the city thought well of them. Day by day, with God's help, their numbers grew. (from Acts 2:45–6)

He (Jesus) went about doing good and healing all that were oppressed by the devil; for God was with him. And we are witnesses to all that he did both in the country of the Jews and in Jerusalem. They put him to death by hanging him upon a tree; but God raised him on the third day and made him manifest, not to all the people, but to us who were chosen by God as witnesses, who ate and drank with him after he rose from the dead. (Acts 10:38–41)

For I delivered to you as of first importance what I also received, that Christ died for our sins in accordance with the scriptures, that he was buried, that he was raised on the third day according to the scriptures, and that he appeared to Cephas, then to the twelve. Then he appeared to more than five hundred brethren at one time, most of whom are still alive, though some have fallen asleep. Then he appeared to James, then to all the apostles. Last of all . . . he appeared to me . . . (Paul's First Letter to the Corinthians 15:3–9

I therefore, a prisoner in the Lord, beg you to lead a life worthy of the calling to which you have been called, with all lowliness and meekness, with patience, forbearing one another in love . . . Let everyone speak truth to his neighbour . . . do not let the sun go down on your anger . . . forgiving one another, as God in Christ forgave you. Therefore be imitators of God, as beloved children. And walk in love, as Christ loved us and gave himself up for us. (Paul to the People of Ephesus, chapter 4)

From the evidence of the above extracts, what answers do you think Christians would give to the following questions:
(a) What kind of person was Jesus? What kind of life did he lead?
(b) How did he die?
(c) What happened after his death to confirm them as his followers, and change his apparent failure into triumph? How certain were they of this?
(d) What effect did their belief seem to have on the way they tried to live their everyday lives?
(e) Did they believe that Jesus was important only to their own nation, the Jews, or that all men of whatever race were called to be his followers and join his fellowship?
Support every one of your answers by close reference to the Christian writings quoted above.

## Christians in Rome

The first Christians were convinced that what they believed about Jesus made such a difference to life that it should be known to everyone. Therefore they preached it. Though they had neither money nor influence behind them (*Not many of you were wise according to earthly standards, not many were powerful, not many of noble birth* . . . wrote Paul to the Christians of Corinth) their numbers grew, and they were soon to be found living their special way of life in most of the larger towns of Asia Minor and Greece. Before twenty years were out they were in Italy, in the capital of the Empire, Rome. We know the names of some of the Roman Christians; they are listed in Paul's Letter to the Romans, chapter 16. Among them are Ampliatur, Urbanus, Stachys, Apelles, the family of Aristobulus ... Philologus, Julia, Nereus and his sister, and Olympas ... The total list is a long one, and contains both Greek and Roman names. Among the Christians of Rome was the great Christian missionary, Paul, who came to Rome as a prisoner about AD 60. Later, Peter, the leader of the close followers of Jesus, came from Antioch in Syria (where the believers in Jesus were first called Christians) to live in Rome.

They did not have it easy. Their fellow-Jews resisted their preaching, and the more educated Greeks were not interested. But things were most difficult for them in Rome. The Roman Empire could not easily tolerate groups of people who did not conform to the usual way of behaving. So many different peoples and races lived within its boundaries that it was always in danger of splitting up. To keep them all together, the authorities promoted the personality-cult of the emperor, and forced all subject peoples to worship him as a god.

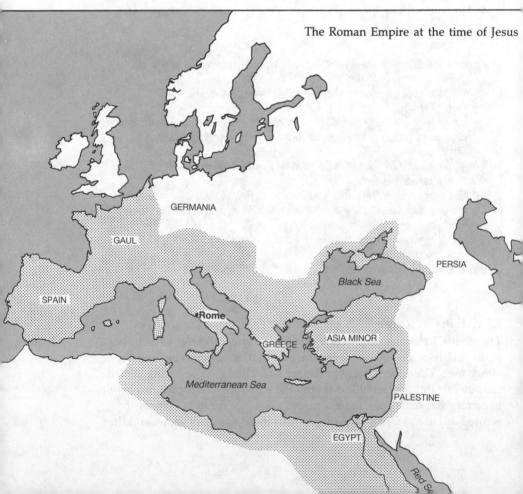

The Roman Empire at the time of Jesus

They constantly had trouble with the Jews over this. But the Jews in Rome were wealthy, and for economic reasons the authorities hesitated to use severe measures against them. The Christians were equally obstinate in their refusal to worship the emperor. They had no influence or protection, and seemed easy victims. Their growing numbers were a threat. Using the pretext of the fire, Nero launched a campaign of violence against them which grew into a total persecution. Their two leaders, Peter and Paul, were among the hundreds who lost their lives, often in terrible ways (Peter is said to have been crucified upside-down). It is against this background that the first gospel, the gospel according to Mark, was written.

## What is a gospel?

The easy answer would seem to be 'a life of Jesus Christ.' In reality this is just what a gospel is not. This does not mean that a gospel tells us nothing about the life of Jesus of Nazareth. But it does mean that Mark (for instance) did not set out to write a biography. A biography generally describes the physical appearance of its hero, gives us details of his early life, and describes his character. Mark does no such thing in his gospel. It is surprising how many things we do not know about Jesus of Nazareth. Was he tall or short, fair or dark, athletic or studious?

We can deduce certain things from what he did. For example, the fact that he could walk into a synagogue and read aloud without preparation (see Luke 4:16–19) means that he could read, and therefore must have been educated. But none of the gospels tells us how or where. And we certainly have no chronologically-ordered account of his life. No: to think of the gospels as biographies is to misunderstand them.

Take the gospel according to Mark. Mark does not say he is writing *the life of Jesus Christ*, but *the good news about Jesus Christ the Son of God* (Mk 1:1). That is why we call what he wrote not a biography, but a GOSPEL (from the Anglo-Saxon words *gōd spel* = good news), and we call the author, not a biographer, but an *evangelist* (from two Greek words meaning: *announcer of good news*).

What *good news* could possibly comfort the Christians of Rome in their helplessness when the whole power of Rome was turned against them? Mark knows that the one thing he can do to help is to reaffirm, to underline, the faith by which every Christian lives, a faith which the Roman community had received from men like Paul and Peter. It was the belief that Jesus was risen by the power of God, and that the new life into which he had entered enabled him to be present among them by his spirit dwelling in their hearts. In this spirit Christians would find courage to remain true to the way of life – a way of truth and love – which they had learned from him; and to remain true to it, if necessary, even to death.

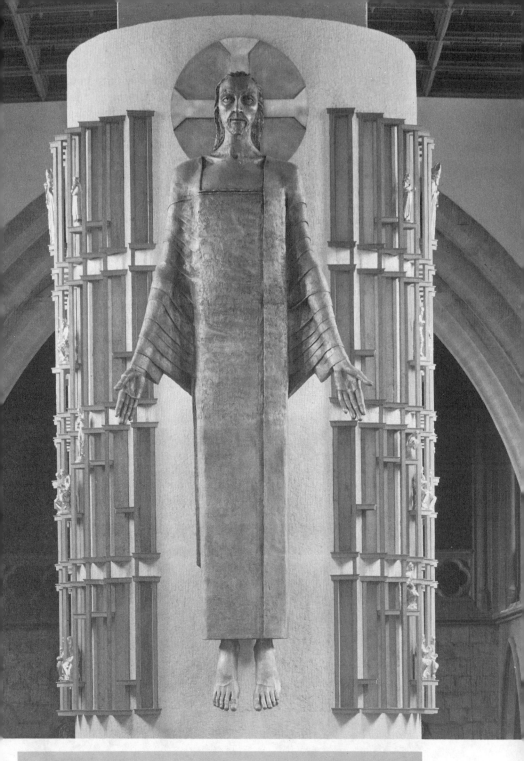

Look at these pictures of Jesus as portrayed by various artists or actors. Which one corresponds most closely to your image of Jesus Christ? Why do you think they are so varied?

So the *good news* Mark wanted to declare was his faith in Christ the Lord. But this glorified *Christ* is the same person as the *Jesus* of Nazareth, who in his earthly life had himself lived the way of truth and love even though it led him to the cross.

So Mark decided that the best way to declare his faith in *Christ* was to re-tell events in the life of *Jesus of Nazareth*, but re-tell them in such a way as to show revealed in these events *Christ the Lord* as he had become known to them in the resurrection.

## A double image

It is as though Mark, in his gospel, places *two pictures* one on top of another:

(a) the picture of *Jesus*, the carpenter of Nazareth, who for three years left his quiet life in Nazareth to live as a wandering preacher, came into conflict with the authorities and died a criminal's death;

(b) the picture of the *Lord Christ*, whom *God had raised up*, the *holy and righteous one*, in whose name all are called to be saved.

And these two pictures are placed, not side by side, but one on top of the other, because Jesus *is* the Christ, the Son of God. The double image which results is what we call a GOSPEL.

Look back at the images of Jesus illustrated on pp. 16–17. Which one for you represents most closely *Jesus, the carpenter of Nazareth*? Which one suggests most the *Lord Christ* image? Discuss what happens when you place the two pictures side by side.

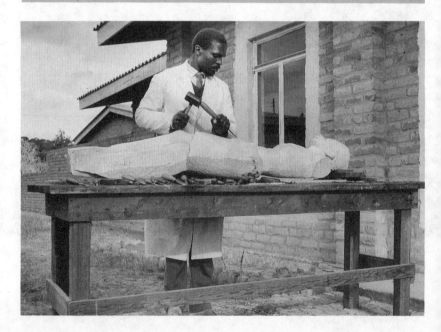

*Note* This is not the only way in which the gospels have been understood. For a long time most people thought of them as faithful accounts of what Jesus did and said. The gospels are full of vivid stories, and many details of geography and history have been confirmed by research and archaeological discoveries. On the other hand, the gospels do not read like straightforward biographies; and the four gospels differ on a number of points. So it has proved impossible to construct from the four gospels a detailed and coherent *Life of Jesus*.

Some people then went to the other extreme. They concluded that the gospels are composed of stories made up by preachers in the early Church, or by the gospel-writers, to express their faith in Christ and their understanding of who he was; and that as a result it was impossible to know anything about what Jesus said and did. This would explain the differences between the gospels. But on the other hand it is clear that from the earliest times Christianity was not just a belief in ideas (as is Marxism, for example), but belief in and love of a person, Jesus of Nazareth who became the Christ. Moreover none of the enemies of Christianity in the first centuries ever attacked the gospels as not being founded in history.

This book takes up a position between these two extremes. It maintains (as do the great majority of experts today) that in the gospels there are true memories of what Jesus said and did, and that these memories are given meaning by the faith of the writer and of the Christian community for which he wrote. So that what the gospels give us is *both* an impression of Jesus's personality and teaching, *and* an insight into what he has come to mean to men and women of all ages. When you have worked through this book you will be better able to judge for yourselves whether this position makes sense.

# 2 The gospel-writers at work

**Where did the gospel-writers get their material?**

The notion of the gospel as a double image (see above) is not easy to grasp. It helps if we consider where the evangelists got their material from. What were their sources? Where did they get their information and their ideas? Out of their own heads? ... From other people? ... From books? ...

They had a number of sources to draw upon.

(a) Memories – their own or others' – of the life of Jesus.

(b) Their experience as Christians of living by the spirit of Jesus in the Christian community, and their contact with those (e.g. Peter) who were among the first witnesses of the resurrection. This was very important. This – that he is risen – is a very central part of the Good News. Moreover, it transformed their memories of Jesus and helped them to see the events of his life in a new way.

(c) The stories told about Jesus by preachers in the early Church, to help people to understand Jesus better and encourage them to live in his way. Many of these stories had become well-known to the Christians.

(d) An early collection of the *Sayings of Jesus*, probably written when the first disciples of Jesus were disappearing through death.

(e) Possibly earlier 'Lives of Jesus'. Most scholars think that Mark wrote his gospel first, and that it was used as one of their sources by Matthew and Luke. This is the point of view followed in this book. Others think that Matthew's was first, and was used by Mark and Luke. (For the evidence either way, see p. 104.)

## How did the gospel-writers handle their material?

Each one according to his purpose.

Because the gospels of Mark, Matthew and Luke have so much of their material in common, they are called the *synoptic* gospels (from two Greek words meaning a *together-view* or a *look-alike*). If this suggests that they were written from the same point of view, the word is misleading. Each evangelist, as we shall see, had his own point of view, and wrote for a particular reading public, with particular problems in mind, and with his own particular emphasis.

Look up Matthew 18: 12–14 and Luke 15: 3–7. They tell the same story. But the endings are different. Look at Matthew's conclusion: who is being spoken to? Look at Luke's conclusion: who is being encouraged?

The difference is explained by the purpose of each writer. Matthew throughout his gospel is concerned with the organisational problems of the early Church. He therefore uses the parable to warn Church leaders of their responsibility for those in their care. *It is not the will of my Father who is in heaven that one of these little ones should perish* (Matt. 18:14). Luke, on the other hand, throughout his gospel wants to stress the mercy of God as revealed in Jesus, and how all men can come to him. He shows how Jesus made himself available even to the outcasts of society; how he was criticised for this; and how this parable justifies him. For *there will be more joy in heaven over one sinner* ... (Lk. 15:7) Details like this help us to see what the particular purpose of each evangelist is.

## Beads on a thread

We can also see it in the way they arrange their material. None of the evangelists tries to arrange the various stories, sayings, etc. into a smooth narrative. Often, a paragraph seems to stand on its own, without any obvious relationship to the one which goes before it or the one which comes after. It has been said that the various stories are like beads which may once have been part of a necklace, but the thread has broken, and they have been scattered all over the floor, then picked up and re-strung haphazardly, without any particular order.

But a closer look shows that there is a kind of order. It is not the order of events in time, but there is certainly an arrangement. Sometimes the arrangement is what we call a *catch-word* one: two stories (or three or more) follow each other because they hinge on the same word, and so one recalls the other to the memory (e.g. look up Mark 12:41–4, where the story of the widow's coins is obviously linked to the word *widows* in verse 40). But more often the order is created by the evangelist in order to say what he wants to say to his reader. The order is part of the message, and is important. Each evangelist rethreads the beads into his own necklace pattern, and the pattern itself may have a meaning.

Look up the Morse alphabet. Can you interpret the message given by the beads in the last photograph? Can you imagine a circumstance in which someone might use this method of attracting attention to his plight?

## The pattern has meaning

We do not need to read far in the gospels to see the evangelist at work in this way. It is sufficient to take the first fourteen verses of the gospel according to Mark.

Mark's gospel opens with the words: *The beginning of the Gospel of Jesus Christ, the Son of God.* The word *gospel* means *good news,* remember. Some translations keep it this way: *The beginning of the good news about Jesus Christ the Son of God.* Mark makes clear from this, the title of his gospel, what he wants to write about.

### Mark's introduction

The first fourteen *verses* of the first chapter are a preface to the whole gospel. In them we read about
    A. John the Baptist
    B. The baptism of Jesus
    C. The temptation in the desert.

**A. John the Baptist** Judging from the four gospels and the typical sermons which are in the Acts of the Apostles, whenever the story was told of Jesus's life, suffering and death, and resurrection it began with a reference to John the Baptist. Mark begins with a quotation.

Just as when you hear the first words or the chorus of a pop song, you are expected to remember the whole song, so Mark expects his readers to remember the whole song from Isaiah. We are less familiar with the Old Testament than were the first-century Christians, so the whole song is written out below. It was composed when the People of God were in exile in Babylon after the Babylonian armies had destroyed their capital city Jerusalem in 586 and had deported them.

GOOD NEWS!
  (The song of the prophet Isaiah)
  The Road Home.
Our slavery is over.
  'Comfort, comfort my people,'
  says your God.
'Speak to the heart of Jerusalem,
  tell her
    her slavery is over,
      her penalty paid
      she has suffered, under God
      full measure for her sins.'
*The Voice*: Listen! Someone is calling!
  Build God's road
    across the wastelands –
  clear a highway for our God
  across the desert.
Valleys shall be raised,
  Mountain and hill levelled out,
rough ground and rugged heights
  smoothed to a plain.
God's glory will dawn
  and the whole world stand in its light,
    God himself has spoken . . .
Climb the Olive Hill
  herald of Good News to Zion!
Shout with all your strength
  herald of good news to Jerusalem!
Shout aloud –
  there's nothing to fear –
    shout to all the Southern cities
'Look – your God.'

            (trans. Alan Dale *The Winding Quest*, pp. 283–4)

Mark understands this song now (since he has known the Risen Christ) as a 'flash-forward', an anticipation of, the joy of the Christian who has seen the coming of God in Jesus. For Mark, therefore, John the Baptist is the herald mentioned in the last verse.

Mark does not tell us much about the teaching of John the Baptist. He concentrates more on his person, on the picture of John as the joyful, prophetic herald.

John appears *in the wilderness* (Mk 1:4). He dresses in the skin of the camel, a desert beast, and eats the food that is to be found in the desert. He is very much a man of the wilderness.

This identification of John with the wilderness is no accident, no mere geographical reference, but part of Mark's message in this preface to his gospel. We need to know how the phrase would sound in the ears of the first-century Christians; and since the Christian church grew out of the Jewish church and inherited much of its tradition, this means knowing how it would sound in the ears of a Jew of Jesus's time.

Phrases become very rich in meaning when they express and recall something important which has been lived through. For men who had fought in the 1914–18 war *the trenches* was such a phrase. It brought back so many experiences, most of them horrible beyond words, but some of them rich in friendship or heroism, which they could never really describe. Only those who had actually shared in this experience would know all that it meant. The word *blitz* has a similar feel about it for the people who were living in London during the Second World War. It recalls days (and especially nights) of terror and deep grief, but which are remembered too for the companionship and the kindness and the courage which belonged to this experience.

For the Jews of Jesus's day and the first-century Christians the phrase *the wilderness* was just such a phrase. They had had two great wilderness experiences in their history. The first was literally a desert experience, when they had wandered for forty years in the desert of Sinai after escaping from Egypt. It was a hard experience; they were hungry and thirsty, and most of those who left Egypt died out there in the wilderness, and never reached the Promised Land. Yet at the same time it was an experience in which they had felt themselves very close to God. His goodness had provided them with food and water in the desert – and at this they never ceased to wonder. Under the leadership of Moses they had been drawn closer to each other and had really felt themselves a people. And they had learned tremendous things about God and their relationship to him which were summed up in the great manifestation of God on Mount Sinai and the giving of the ten commandments. So the wilderness had become in their memory a place of hardship and humiliation in which they had yet known what it means to be saved by God.

Their second wilderness experience was the time when they had been carried off into captivity into Babylon. They were not literally in the desert this time, but it was like the desert wanderings all over again. They were displaced persons. Far away from their own country, their great city and temple of Jerusalem lying in ruins, they felt alone and forsaken. Yet they were not lost among these strangers, but managed to keep their national identity and to understand, as they had never understood before, how God had been present to them right through their history and was present to them still. Once again, in hardship and humiliation they had known what it means to be saved by God; which is why they often spoke afterwards of their Babylonian captivity as a stay in the *wilderness*.

And now it becomes clear why Mark wants to present John the Baptist as a *man of the wilderness*. History repeats itself. In the life and death of Jesus of Nazareth, especially in the hardship and humiliation of his suffering and death (a *wilderness* experience of being at once abandoned by and near to God) salvation will finally come to men; and to Mark it is fitting that a shout of joy out of the wilderness should announce it.

**B. The Baptism of Jesus (Mk 1:9–11)**  Mark chooses to record only four things about this incident in the life of Jesus:
(a) that Jesus was baptised in the Jordan by John;
(b) that he *saw the heavens opened*;
(c) that the Spirit, like a dove, descended on him; and
(d) that he heard a voice from heaven.
These are all clues to Mark's message about Jesus.
(a) Jesus was baptised by John in the Jordan. This links Jesus's teaching with John's, and helps the reader to see him as the one John was referring to when he said: *After me comes one who is mightier than I* (Mk 1:7).
(b) He saw *the heavens opened*: this among the Jews was a standard way of expressing a moment of communication between God and man. It could mean what we mean when we say: 'In prayer he understood . . .'.
(c) and (d): The *Spirit descending* and the voice saying *Thou art my beloved Son: with thee I am well pleased* are meant to recall to the reader another song from the Old Testament, from Isaiah 42:1–4:

> Here is my servant (or son) whom I uphold,
> my chosen one in whom my soul delights.
> I have endowed him with my spirit
> that he may bring true justice to the nations.
> He does not cry out or shout aloud
> or make his voice heard in the streets.
> He does not break the crushed reed
> nor quench the wavering flame.
> Faithfully he brings true justice,
> he will neither waver, nor be crushed
> until true justice is established on earth,
> for the islands are awaiting his law.

This passage, and many like it, were thought of by the Jews as announcing the Saviour who was to come. Mark sees them fulfilled in Jesus.

**C. The temptation in the wilderness**  Mark does little more than refer to a story about Jesus which the other evangelists tell at greater length. What is important for Mark is: that it takes place in the wilderness; that it is an encounter with evil; and that Jesus finally overcomes. It is a kind of summary of Jesus's whole life.

In fact, these first thirteen verses together make up a summary of the whole of Mark's gospel. It is like a musical overture in which the themes of the whole opera occur and are interwoven. Mark shows Jesus as the one who brings joy to men by fulfilling all the expectations of the Old Testament. He is in communion with God. Strong in the fullness of God's spirit which rests in him, he enters the wilderness of life, meets the evil which is mingled with all human experience, conquers it and brings salvation to men. This, for Mark, summarises the Good News of Jesus Christ the Son of God. In this the Christians of Rome were to find courage and hope.

**Chapter and verse**

On p. 22 you were advised to look up Mark 12:41–4. The first figure (12) is the number of the chapter; after the colon you find the numbers of the verses.

None of the books of the Bible was divided into chapter and verse by the men who wrote them. They have been divided that way since, to make it easier to refer to a particular passage and look it up.

The four gospels were first divided into chapters by an Englishman, Stephen Langton, who was Archbishop of Canterbury from 1207 to 1228. The idea was backed up by a French cardinal, Hugh de Cher, in 1240, and became universal when it was used in the first printed edition of the Bible in Latin.

The division into verses was the work of a famous French printer, Henri Etienne, in 1551. It made reference to Bible texts so easy that all printers have used it since.

# MARK

---

# 3 Call and response: a man with authority (Mk 1:14–3:6)

---

### Galilee of the Gentiles

This whole section is set either in Galilee itself or in the non-Jewish areas north or east of Galilee. Many scholars think that this geographical location in itself is part of Mark's message.

*God does not have favourites*

One of the difficulties for anyone coming to Christianity from the Jewish tradition was to accept that Christ's message and the life of his spirit was as much for the non-Jew as for the Jew. We have a good deal of evidence that the first preachers of the gospel did not find it easy to understand that Jesus's mission and his message were for all men. They had been brought up to think of Jews as very special, and still tended to think that Jesus had come only for Jews. Those who knew Jesus better understood better. To quote from the words of Peter in a famous sermon: *The truth I have come to realise is that God does not have favourites, but anybody of any nationality who fears God and does what is right is acceptable to him.* (Acts of the Apostles, 10:34, *Jerusalem Bible trans.*) It was particularly important for Mark to make this clear, since the Church in Rome for which he was writing was largely composed of gentile (i.e. non-Jewish) converts.

And so Mark makes great use of traditions which speak of Jesus as born in Nazareth (in Galilee) and teaching and working in Galilee. For Galilee was not as 'Jewish' as Judaea; the people of Galilee were of mixed race, so that Galilee was sometimes called *Galilee of the Gentiles*. Mark shows that the despised Galilee, the land of the gentiles, is the place where salvation appears. There Jesus is received by the poor and the outcast, whereas the official representatives of the Jewish faith oppose him from the beginning, and it is in Jerusalem of Judaea that he finally suffers and dies.

In this dramatic way Mark shows that God's love and salvation are offered to all men. He underlines this also by stories in which Jesus is shown meeting gentiles and accepting their faith in him.

## A man with authority (1:14–3:6)

In this section Mark has woven together three 'calling' stories; four 'curing and teaching' stories; and four 'argument' stories.

(a) *The three 'calling' stories.* These are:

the calling of Simon and his brother Andrew (1:16–18);
the calling of James and his brother John (1:19–20);
the calling of Levi, son of Alphaeus (2:13–14).

These stories are very briefly told. They all emphasise how promptly Jesus's call was obeyed. Simon and Andrew left their nets *immediately* and followed Jesus. *Immediately* he called James and John, who left their father in the boat and followed him. Levi the son of Alpheus *got up from his desk* in the tax-office and followed him. So Jesus appears in all these stories as one whose word has authority over people.

These incidents are also important because the men named here are among those who followed Jesus during the whole of his public life, and became, after his resurrection, leaders in the Church. They are called *apostles* (from a Greek word meaning *sent*). They were not chosen from among the important people of Galilee: four were fishermen, and Levi (probably the same person as 'Matthew' – see the gospel according to Matthew (9:9)) – was a customs officer, from a class despised by the good Jew (see p. 34).

(b) *The 'curing-and-teaching' stories*

Four 'cures' are told by Mark:

the cure of a man with *an unclean spirit* (1:23–8);
the cure of Simon's mother-in-law (1:29–31);
the cure of a leper (1:40–45);
the cure of a paralysed man (2:1–12)

Also in 1:32–4 there is a picture of many people coming to Jesus for healing.

The Jews of Jesus's time knew much less about how the body works than we do. Illness was to them very mysterious, and it was obviously bad; so it belonged to all that part of man's experience which we call *evil*. In particular, leprosy (which contaminated people and made them unfit to mix with others) and paralysis (which makes a person helpless and unfree) were images of sin. Also, any physical or mental state which was strange and terrifying and inexplicable (which we would diagnose, for example, as schizophrenia or epilepsy), a first-century Jew would think must be due to possession by an evil spirit.

How were the mentally sick treated in the England of Shakespeare's day? (see *Twelfth Night*: the treatment of Malvolio). Do you know anything about the change in attitudes to and understanding of mental illness in the last hundred years? What differences would you expect to find between a mental hospital built at the beginning of the century and a new one? Do you know anything about community care of the mentally sick?

The full meaning of the miracle stories in the gospels will be discussed more fully in chapter 3. For the moment we note:

 (i) that they are closely linked with the teaching of Jesus (see 1:22 and 27)
 (ii) that they again emphasise the authority of Jesus: authority to teach (1:22); to overcome evil (1:27); to forgive sin (2:11); and show it as an authority which raises men up and makes them whole;
(iii) that they are received enthusiastically by the Galilean crowds (make a note for yourselves of all the places where this is expressed).

(c) *The 'argument' stories*

*Note* To understand these we need to know something about certain groups of people who appear in the gospel narrative. The following are those who feature in this section.

**The Herodians**: Palestine at the time of Jesus was part of the Roman Empire. The Romans governed most of their colonies indirectly, that is, through local 'kings' set up by and accountable to them. In the period immediately before the birth of Jesus the whole of Palestine had been governed by King Herod the Great. His policy was one of conciliation. On the one hand he felt and acted like a Jew, and would not allow anything in his kingdom which would upset the religious feelings of the Jews. He would not allow, for example, any portrait of Caesar to be brought into Jerusalem, since the Jews would have associated this with the worship of the emperor as a god; nor would he allow any coins to be minted with Caesar's head on them – though this was done after Herod's death. He improved the city of Jerusalem and rebuilt the Temple.

On the other hand, Herod appreciated what the civilisation of Greece and Rome had to offer, and encouraged the Jews to accept Roman ways in recreation, sport etc.

Many people thought that his attitude was a wise one; and these were the Herodians spoken of in the gospels. They were prepared to accept Roman political power if they could be free to practise their religion. Herod's attitude seemed to guarantee this, and to discourage troublemakers.

**The Pharisees** were different. They were very devout Jews. For them the law of Moses was sacred. It represented the Will of God, and had to be kept in every detail; to break it was sinful. So afraid were they of breaking the law that they made a hedge around it of other laws, which were meant to make quite sure that you did not get near breaking God's law. For example, the Saturday of each week was the sabbath or day of rest, when Jews were forbidden by Moses's law to work; and it began on Friday evening at 6 p.m. To make sure that you did not forget when six o'clock came, and therefore break the sabbath laws in the first half-hour, the Pharisees suggested that good Jews ought to begin their sabbath on Friday morning. Such extra laws are generally called *traditions* in the gospels.

The Pharisees do not get a good press in the gospels. They are shown as so keen on *traditions* that they forget the really important things, like kindness to others, openness and generosity. But this is not the complete picture. They were very loyal to their nation and to their God. They had kept the people faithful to God when even the priestly leaders had become selfish and materialistic; and after Jerusalem was destroyed in AD 70 they led a great religious revival among the remnant of the Jews. 'Good' Pharisees are mentioned in the gospels (Nicodemus and Joseph of Arimathea), and one of the greatest followers of Jesus in the early Church, Paul, had been brought up as a fervent Pharisee.

Though the Pharisees were anti-Roman, they did not favour violence nor preach open rebellion. They advocated only non-violent resistance, and religious fidelity.

**The Zealots**: Since the death of Herod the Great there had existed in Palestine, sometimes openly and sometimes underground, a resistance movement which believed in the use of violence to overthrow Roman rule. Its members were called Zealots. Because they believed that they must stop at nothing, not even at assassination, to gain their ends, and because their weapons were not bombs, but daggers, they later became known as 'dagger-men'. One of the apostles seems to have been one of them (see Mk 3:19).

Quote some examples of (a) violent, (b) non-violent resistance you have read of in the papers. What do you think about terrorist action? Do you think that the use of violence is ever justified to free men from oppression? Do you know anything of the non-violent resistance of Ghandi and of Martin Luther King?

**The rabbis** were men who had studied both the law of Moses and all the traditions. Their job was to tell the people what was forbidden by the law and to interpret it. (For example, what exactly was meant by 'working' on the sabbath? Was travelling 'working', and if so, how long a journey made it 'travel'? Could you go half a mile? One mile? Six miles? . . . And were you allowed to fight on the sabbath? And if not, what were you supposed to do if you were attacked by muggers? and so on . . .).                                                                (cont'd)

**Tax-collectors** are also mentioned in this section. The Jews had to pay two kinds of taxes to the Romans: a land-tax and a poll-tax (i.e. so much per head). There were also custom dues to be paid when you passed from one Roman province to another. (For example, Capernaum on the sea of Galilee was a frontier town between the province ruled by Herod Antipas and the one ruled by his half-brother Philip. Therefore there was a customs post at Capernaum. See Mk 2:14.)

The Romans did not collect these taxes themselves from the people, but they employed local men to do this for them. Each tax-collector was responsible for handing on a fixed sum to the Romans. If what he collected was less than this, he had to make it up out of his own pocket; if it was more, he could keep the balance. Naturally, the tax-collectors made sure it would be more. They were very unpopular because they often made people pay very high taxes so that they would have plenty left over for themselves. They were also unpopular because they were working for the hated Romans; and because the coins they handled, the coins of the tax-money, were Roman coins with the head of Caesar on them – which the Jews thought was a kind of idolatry.

Tax-collectors were therefore looked down on by everybody, and no respectable Jew would be seen with one of them. That is why people were so shocked that Jesus actually went into their homes and ate with them.

Twelve or fifteen members of the class go aside and divide themselves (not necessarily equally) into Herodians, Pharisees, Zealots, rabbis and tax-collectors. The other members of the class do not know to which group each belongs.

Now imagine the following situation in Jerusalem: news has come that the Roman governor of the city intends to melt down some of the sacred vessels from the Temple so as to finance improvements to the sanitation of the poorer parts of the city. Help each other to work out how your group would feel about this: e.g. if you are a 'Pharisee' work out with the other 'Pharisees' what your attitude would be.

Back in class, another pupil interviews you, trying to discover the views of your group. From your answers, the rest of the class try to guess to which group you belong. (NB You win if they guess – not if they don't.)

We are now in a position to understand what the four 'argument' stories are all about.

### The argument about eating with sinners (2:15–17)

This is easy in the light of the information given above. Mark links it naturally with the call of Levi, who as a customs officer would rank as a tax-collector. Jesus eats with such people; he is criticised for this; and defends himself with the saying, obviously treasured by the early Church, about the sick needing a doctor (and the sinner needing a saviour).

## The argument about fasting (2:18–22)

This is more complicated. Scholars think that this story may have grown as the experience of Christians led them to think about the question of fasting (which is important in Jewish law).

Maybe it can be taken to pieces as follows:

(i) Jesus seems from the gospels to have enjoyed the good things of life and not to have been afraid of having fun. Perhaps at the heart of this story is the memory of a day when he had recommended feasting instead of fasting on a particular occasion. (*Can the wedding-guests fast when the bridegroom is with them*? v. 19)

(ii) The early Christians remembered these words of Jesus, and used them to defend themselves when they were criticised for not observing the Jewish feasts as did the disciples of John and the Pharisees. This, built into the story, would give us verse 18: *Why do John's disciples and the disciples of the Pharisees fast, but your disciples do not fast*?

(iii) Later still the Christians themselves took up again the practice of fasting. Hearing (or reading) the story told in verses 18–19 they would remember that *bridegroom* was an image sometimes used of Christ, and they would say: 'Yes, that was all right when the bridegroom (Jesus) was with us, but now that he has been taken from us (and has returned to the Father) we must fast.' Putting all this together, we get verses 18–20 as they now stand. If the passage has grown up like this, it is an interesting illustration of how the traditions which went into the making of the gospel were moulded by the faith and the reflection and the life of the early Church.

In any case, the two comparisons which follow emphasise the claim Jesus seems to be making that there is something in the Good News which is really new, and which is more important than religious practices, however good.

The first comparison is one which a woman of those days would understand (2:21). We do not do much patching nowadays: but when you did patch linen or cotton, you knew that if you patched an old garment with a new piece of material, the new piece would shrink in the wash and tear the material all round the patch.

The second comparison (2:22) belongs to what was a man's world. Wine bottles in Jesus's day were made of leather. They were valuable and were used over and over again. But they tended in the end to wear thin and become brittle. Obviously the fermenting power of new wine could strain to bursting point any old bottles. So for new wine, new skins! In other words, the power and the freshness of the spirit which Jesus would give to men could not be contained in the regulations of the Jewish (or any other) law.

## The argument about plucking ears of corn on the sabbath (2:23–8)

The strict Pharisees (building hedges around the law) would interpret this as reaping, which was forbidden on the sabbath day. Jesus argues from the Old Testament – a way of proving your point very familiar to the rabbis. He shows that David did not hesitate to break the law when he and his followers were hungry. Man's need justifies the breaking of this kind of law.

The story serves to build up to the conclusion that *the sabbath was made for man, and not man for the sabbath*, which was easy to remember. Mark also sees Jesus's judgement on this matter as another example of his authority, and adds: *So the Son of Man is Lord even of the sabbath.*

### The argument about curing on the sabbath (3:1–6)

The way in which Mark tells this story gives us the impression that the teaching and actions of Jesus have already aroused strong opposition among certain powerful people, who have made up their minds about him (see especially 3:2). The situation is presented as a kind of trap. Jesus takes up the challenge by showing once again that law is for life, not death.

> Why does every society need law? What is law for? In what kind of circumstances might it be good for a man to break the law? Are there any laws in our society which you think should be changed? Which and why?

## Conclusion

The section (1:15 to 3:6) studied in this chapter is again a kind of mini-gospel. Jesus calls men to follow him; goes about doing good and manifesting the kingdom of love; is rejected by men and condemned to death.

In this section, too, Mark emphasises above all the authority of Jesus. The faith of the early Christians was such that Christ was the authority which governed their lives; his teaching was the rule by which they lived, his law of love was their law. They knew from their experience that fidelity to this law and this love could mean death. Mark shows that it was so with Jesus.

> The photograph on this page shows Mother Teresa speaking to the World Synod of Bishops of the Roman Catholic Church (Oct. 1980) The Pope, who holds the highest authority in that Church, is listening to her, recognising the authority with which she speaks. Present, besides the bishops, were people who had been invited as authorities in their particular fields.
>
> What does the word *authority* mean in each of these cases? Who or what gives authority to certain people? What is *authoritarianism*? In whom do *you* recognise authority?

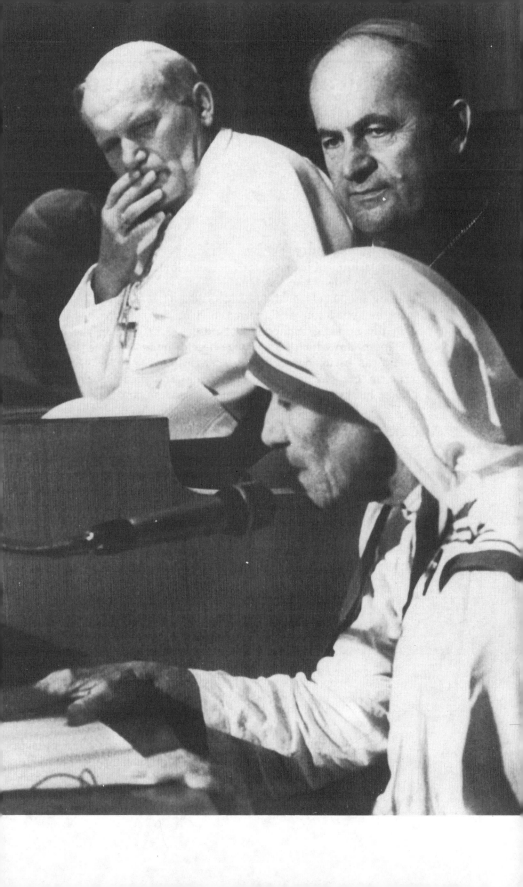

# 4 Call and response: those who believed (Mk 3:7–6:6)

## Into pagan country

The preaching of Jesus so far has been limited to a very small area. Mark has shown him teaching

    along the shores of the Sea of Galilee (1:16–2:13)

    in the synagogue at Capernaum (1:21; 3:1)

    in the house of Simon and Andrew (1:29) and in the house at Capernaum which seems to be his, for he is 'at home' there (2:15) and can invite people in to eat with him.

True, in 1:38–45 he goes further afield and preaches *throughout all Galilee*, but he comes back again to Capernaum, and it is to the people of Galilee that he speaks throughout.

Verse 7 of chapter 3 marks a new beginning. People now come to Jesus from outside Galilee, and some of the districts Mark mentions are beyond the Jordan (i.e. on the east bank) and the region of Tyre and Sidon. These are pagan (i.e. non-Jewish) districts. And before this section is over we shall see Jesus travelling out of Galilee into pagan country.

## Healing to the pagans

In 1:32–4 the reader was given a description of the Galilean crowds coming to Jesus for healing. In 3:7–12 Jesus gives the same encouragement and brings the same wholeness to the crowds of pagans from outside Galilee. It doesn't seem to matter to him where a person comes from; all that counts is that the person is sick and in need.

Find out about the Geneva Convention and the work of the International Red Cross. Can you find anything in the principles of the Red Cross which corresponds with the attitude of Jesus here?

Collect from the newspapers in the weeks ahead any reference to or pictures of Red Cross personnel at work. Make a collage illustrating 'all that counts is that a man is sick and in need.'

## The Messianic secret

A curious feature of Mark's gospel appears for the first time in 3:12. The unclean spirits (that is, the men who appear possessed) proclaim Jesus as the Son of God; and Mark adds *and he strictly ordered them not to make him known*. Why should Jesus say this?

In fact, over and over again in Mark's gospel Jesus tells evil spirits not to make known who he was, and forbids people he has cured to tell others what he has done for them. It seems a strange thing to ask, and a very difficult command to obey, for when we are very happy about something we want to tell everyone. In some cases (look up 5:43) it would seem impossible to hide what had happened. Yet Mark insists on it. He also very often remarks that the disciples failed to understand what Jesus did or said. It is as though Jesus tried to hide who he was, and managed it so successfully that even his disciples did not understand half the time what his actions and his words really meant.

This characteristic of Mark's gospel is called the Messianic secret.

Why is this? Some people think that Jesus did not want to make himself known too soon as the Messiah. He knew that many Jews were expecting the Messiah to lead a liberating army against the Romans, and that if he were labelled as the Messiah too quickly, before he had time to explain what he really stood for, people would expect him to be this kind of nationalist military leader. So he played down his Messiahship until the apostles were more ready to understand it.

But because this is characteristic only of Mark's gospel, some scholars think it is Mark's invention, a literary device used by him to convey an important idea. And their study of the language and style of these passages seems to bear this out.

If it is Mark's invention, why did he want to show Jesus in this way? What was he trying to say?

Several explanations have been suggested:

(a)  At the time when Mark wrote his gospel in Rome, the Jews of Palestine were being very troublesome to the Roman authorities, and several guerrilla leaders had tried to overthrow the Roman regime in Palestine. Mark did not want the Romans to think that Jesus had been that kind of guerrilla leader, so he puts words into Jesus's mouth which make it clear that he was not making a bid for power.

(b)  Or maybe it was the Christians of Rome who were in danger of getting the wrong idea. We know from the Jewish historian Josephus (who died in AD 98) that Jesus had acquired a wide reputation, by the time Mark came to write, as a wonder-worker. But Mark did not want him to be thought of as a common magician, doing wonder-tricks to impress the people. That was not what he was about. So Mark shows Jesus as anxious to avoid giving this impression, which would be false to the nature of his Messiahship.

(c)  Or it could be something to do with the *double image* of Jesus Christ given in the gospel (see p. 18). Mark is convinced, through the resurrection, that Jesus is the Lord. He retells the events of Jesus's life in such a way as to convey his faith in Jesus. It is therefore the glorified Christ whom Mark portrays in the gospel pages walking the roads of Palestine. But *when* he walked the roads of Palestine he was *not* glorified, and people did not recognise him as the Christ. It was difficult for Mark's readers, with their faith in Christ, to understand why his contemporaries did not recognise his lordship. So maybe Mark invented the literary device of the Messianic secret to explain their blindness – or even to suggest to his readers that even they could not understand who Jesus was until they had met the risen Christ in their own lives.

## The apostles (3:13–19)

Mark has already shown (1:16–20) that very early in his public life Jesus called people to follow him in a special way. (Do you remember their names?) Now Mark gives us the names of the twelve men who are to be most closely associated with him. We call them *apostles* (from a Greek word meaning *sent*). Once again the call is authoritative. He called to him, says Mark, *those whom he desired*. The list of twelve is given by all the synoptic gospels, with no variation except that Luke calls Thaddaeus *Jude the brother of James*. To the early Christians the fact that they were twelve was probably very significant because it recalled the twelve sons of Jacob from whom the twelve tribes of Israel were descended.

Look at the names of the twelve apostles. Some you have met before. Write notes on what you know of them. Keep these notes up-to-date as you learn more of them.

Two of them have what we would call surnames, i.e. they are called *son of N.* (Jesus's surname would have been Barjoseph, i.e. son of Joseph). Three of them have nicknames. Why do you think James and John were nicknamed *sons of thunder*? (You will find a clue in Luke 9:54.)

Look up Matthew 16:17–18. Can you tell from this passage what Simon's father's name was, and what the nickname *Peter* means?

## True relationship with Jesus

The next section (3:20–25) is not easy to understand. There is an obvious contrast between the ordinary people on the one hand, who receive Jesus with faith, and on the other hand his own relations and the scribes. (The scribes were originally men who could read and write, and whose job it was to preserve the sacred writings of the Jews by copying, editing and publishing them. By the time of Jesus their familiarity with the sacred writings had made them interpreters of these writings for the ordinary people.) These last two groups might both, for different reasons, have been expected to welcome Jesus, but both attribute his words and actions to the influence of an evil spirit. (To be *beside oneself* or *out of one's mind* was for the Jews the same thing as being possessed of an evil spirit.)

Jesus replies to this accusation with a comparison. Just as a burglar cannot burgle the house of a strong man unless he is powerful enough to make that man helpless, so neither can Jesus deliver men from evil, says Mark, unless he is more powerful in good than the evil spirit is in evil. The idea of Jesus in conflict with the spirit of evil and overcoming it was introduced in the preface (1:13) and is always in the mind of Mark. It could be particularly important to the Christians of Rome, who felt very threatened by the evil power of the Roman imperial authorities.

In this context *blasphemy against the Holy Spirit* would seem to be the obstinate refusal to acknowledge that what Jesus reveals is the goodness of God.

Note on *his mother and his brothers*
There has been from early times a strong tradition among Christians that Mary had no other children but Jesus. The Roman Catholic Church and the Eastern Church in particular continue to hold this tradition. They point out that the words *brother* and *sister* were used easily among the Jews (as they are e.g. among African peoples today) of any close blood relations, e.g. cousins. Others, however, think that there is no reason why we should not understand these words as they are commonly meant; and that their use by Mark indicates that the tradition that Jesus was Mary's only child only arose after Mark's gospel was written.

## Parables

Mark continues to encourage his readers by the message of hope contained in the five parables which follow.

A parable is a simile (or comparison) which has been developed into a story. Instead of simply saying: *The life of God within us is precious and hidden, like hidden treasure,* one might say: *It is as though there were a treasure hidden in a field. And a man* . . . and we make up a story to bring out the preciousness and hiddenness of God's life in us.

The stories Jesus told, his parables, are simple stories taken from the everyday life of the people among whom he lived; but they have an inner meaning. Most parables make only one point; in this a parable is different from an **allegory**. In an allegory every detail helps to spell out the hidden meaning, whereas in a parable the details merely build up the story, and the main point gives the hidden meaning.

The first of Mark's parables is the Parable of the Sower (4:1–20). Its background is the farming life of Palestine. Seed was sown by simply scattering it with a wide sweep of the arm; we call it *sowing broadcast*. Obviously it was less accurate than modern methods. Moreover in Palestine the seed was often sown before the field was ploughed, so that if some seed went on the footpath or among the weeds it would not matter all that much, as both path and weedy patch might be ploughed in when the plough came round. So the man in the parable was not perhaps such a bad sower as he seems.

The parable is followed by an explanation given to *those who were about him with the twelve.* The explanation turns the parable into an allegory. In the allegory the path, the stony ground and the thorns stand for different kinds of people – different in the way they accept God's word. Probably this is not how it was told by Jesus; in the way Jesus told it, it would have only one point: a comparison between the frustrations of the sower's task, when so much of the seed seemed to be wasted, and the triumph of the harvest. Jesus is full of confidence. Although so many of his words seem to have been wasted (see 3:6) he looks forward with joy to the harvest which will surely come. The original lesson of the parable was that in spite of every failure and

opposition, from hopeless beginnings God brings forth the triumphant end which he has promised.

Verses 13–20 show us how this parable came to be used in the early Church. In an attempt to get as much out of it as possible, it is expanded into an allegory, and made to yield a moral lesson on the way in which a man should receive the word if it is to bear fruit in his heart.

The development of the parable in the early Church (verses 13–20) shows four types of people among those to whom the word was preached. Complete this chart:

*Seed on footpath* = people who . . .
*Seed on stony ground* = people who . . .
*Seed among thorns* = people who . . .
*Seed on good soil* = people who . . .

It is sometimes said that these four types are represented in any average group of people, and that the story illustrates how they would react characteristically to any call made upon them. Imagine that a man keen on conservation came to your school and asked your class for volunteers to clear the local canal of weeds and mud, so that it could be used for recreation. Three months later a TV reporter came along to find out how the project had gone, and he interviewed some people in your class, asking what they had done about it. Act out the interview, role-playing four imaginary class-members who have reacted to the situation as did the four types in the parable.

Four short parables follow, three of them bearing the same message of encouragement. The following notes help to understand them:

v. 21    *Lamp* The ordinary house had only one room, lit by a lamp on a stand by the door. Jesus is the lamp.

vv. 24–25    *Measure* The parable may have been included here by 'catch-word' association with *bushel* in verse 21 (see p. 22.)

vv. 27–29    Note all that happens between seed-sowing and harvesting, while the sower is apparently doing nothing.

v. 31    In Jewish proverbs the mustard-seed is referred to as the smallest of all seeds. On the plains of Gennesaret it grows into a plant about three metres high.

> Which three of these four parables convey the same message of encouragement, and which is the odd one out?

## Miracles (4:35–5:43)

The same message of comfort and encouragement is then expressed by Mark in four miracle stories, which show how Jesus brings wholeness to those who respond in faith, and brings order out of chaos. Evil is not overcome without conflict and struggle, but in the end Jesus triumphs. This was Mark's original theme (see p. 27).

It is useful to begin by concentrating on the second of these miracle stories (5:1–20) which at first sight is strange and difficult to understand. The following background notes help:

(a) The *country of the Gerasenes* cannot be exactly located, but the reference is to the eastern shores of the lake. Most of the people living there were non-Jews. This is the first time that Mark shows Jesus going into pagan country.

(b) *The sea*: The Jews were not a sea-faring people, and they feared the sea. They thought of it as the place where demons dwell.

> For much of their history the Jews had no access to the sea, other than the inland sea of Tiberias, otherwise called the Lake of Galilee. During the reign of David and Solomon, the kingdom did extent to a port on the Red Sea – the modern Aquaba – which Solomon made use of to send trading expeditions down the coast of Africa; but when the kingdom disintegrated after his death, there were no further ventures of this kind. For hundreds of years most of the Mediterranean coastlands were in the hands of the enemies of Israel, the Philistines. At the time of Jesus there was one sizeable town, Caesarea, on the Mediterranean coast, but this was a Roman garrison town and pleasure-resort; the real sea-ports, centres of international trade, were Tyre and Sidon in pagan territory to the north.
>
> The way in which the Jews felt about the sea can be gathered from references in the psalms, among them the dramatic description in

(cont'd)

Psalm 107. In this psalm the poet sings abut four groups of people who are particularly miserable and need God's help to rescue them: namely, those who are lost in the desert; prisoners; the sick; and those who are at sea. Of them he writes:

Some went down to the sea in ships,
   doing business in the great waters;
they saw the deeds of the Lord,
   his wondrous works in the deep.
For he commanded, and raised the stormy winds,
   which lifted up the waves of the sea.
They mounted up to heaven, they went down into the depths;
   their courage melted away in their evil plight,
they reeled and staggered like drunken men
and were at their wits' end.                    (Psalm 107:23–7)

(c) *swine*: The Jews were not allowed to eat pork. The pig was for them an unclean animal; it symbolised sin and evil. Only in pagan country could there be a herd of swine.

(d) *Legion:* This is a Roman military term: a unit of the Roman army made up of six thousand foot-soldiers, a hundred and twenty horsemen, and technical personnel. For the Jews of the time the Roman legions were the occupying army.

(e) *Tombs*: Natural or man-made caves were often used as graves.

A good way to search for the meaning of a gospel story is to read it very carefully, paying close attention to the words used by the writer, the way he builds up his story, his description of persons, his references to places and times, and especially to any contrast he may suggest between the beginning and the end of the story. If we look for the key words in this story we get:

vv. 1–5: *No one could bind him . . . fetters . . . chains . . . wrenched apart . . . broken . . . crying out* (the Greek word suggests inarticulate cries, howling like an animal) *. . . bruising* or *cutting himself with stones . . . night and day . . . tombs . . . mountains.*

vv. 14–20: *sitting . . . clothed . . . in his right mind . . . city . . . country . . . neighbourhood . . . home . . . friends.*

And the watershed between these two sets of words is provided by the exchange of names (*Legion . . . Jesus Son of the Most High God*) and the dramatic picture of the helter-skelter of the herd of swine over the cliffs into the sea.

The contrast is very clear. At the beginning of the story there is this

man, more like an animal than a man, living in wild and weird places, naked, unable to sleep, howling like an animal, wounding his own body, without any sense of identity, not even able to name himself except by a non-name which suggests that he is at odds with himself and does not really know who he is. At the end of the story is a person, sitting, clothed, in his full senses, and able to relate socially, to find himself a home among his own people.

What has transformed him is his meeting with Jesus, Son of the Most High God. There is violence in the meeting: his first words (though at least he finds words, which is already the beginning of becoming human) are violent. But the moment of change in him is marked above all by the violent picture of the great herd of evil animals plunging into the sea. Evil destroys, says Mark; but the man is now whole, and the devils go back to their own place.

The story is important to Mark. At the beginning of his gospel he showed Jesus as the one who *enters the wilderness of life, meets the evil which is mingled with all human experience, conquers it and brings salvation to men* (p. 27). In this story Jesus enters pagan country, in a wild and desolate setting; there he meets the violence of evil in its most destructive form, conquers it dramatically, so that evil takes flight at his approach, and brings salvation to a man. The end-result is not a personal triumph for Jesus – he is in fact rejected – but the man who has been touched by him becomes an apostle and bears witness to what he has received. (He is an exception in that he is not forbidden to talk about it – on the contrary.) The story is like the whole gospel on a small scale.

*Note* The modern reader, coming to this passage for the first time, tends to get sidetracked by the episode of the pigs-over-the-cliff. It seems such a waste of good bacon – and so unfair to the owners of the pigs! It is unlikely that Mark's first readers would have missed, as a modern reader might, the strong symbolism of this picture. It has been suggested that a herd of pigs may have stampeded over a cliff somewhere in this area, that the event was remembered in popular story, and that Mark took this folk-memory and wove it into his narrative to express the violence of evil and its destructive power. We shall probably never know whether this suggestion is well founded; but if it were so, it would be a good example of Mark at work, using his available material to proclaim his message.

The story of the Gerasene demoniac is framed by two other miracle stories: **the calming of the storm** (4:35–41) and **the raising of Jairus's daughter** (5:21–4, 35–43) – ignoring for the moment the story of the woman with a haemorrhage, which is sandwiched into the middle of the Jairus story. If these two miracle stories are read carefully, it appears that they do not come together by accident in Mark's gospel, but follow a common pattern and convey a similar message. Through the three stories, arranged in succession like this, Mark seems to be making an important statement about Jesus. What is it?

Take in turn 4:35–41 and 5:21–4, 35–43.
  For each make a list of key-words in the first half and in the second half of the story, as was done above (p. 46) for the story of the Gerasene demoniac.
  Can you see a contrast between the first half and the second half? Can you find the words which serve as 'watershed'? Can you sum up the teaching contained in each of these stories? Can you see a common pattern? What do you think Mark is telling his readers, through these three stories, about Jesus?

Inserted into the last story (of Jairus) is another, the story of the **woman with a haemorrhage** (5:25–34). Mark has quite a habit of interrupting one story to tell another, and then returning to the first. Here it serves a dramatic purpose: Jesus's journey to the synagogue is held up while he attends to this woman (there is an understandable note of impatience in the words of the disciples) and he arrives at the synagogue too late. The little story itself is vividly told. It becomes more significant if we realise that the illness the woman suffered from would make her unclean in Jewish law, and the pious Jew would consider himself defiled if in a crowd his clothes brushed against her. As on other occasions, Jesus's concern for people frees him from this kind of strict observance. Mark, in telling the story, emphasises how the woman's faith, awakened by her meeting with Jesus, calls forth his healing power.

## Did it really happen?

In reading these four miracle stories, we have been asking what they mean, what Mark is telling his readers through these stories about Jesus and discipleship.

But inevitably the question arises: Did they really happen? Did Jesus really cure people at a word and raise people from the dead, or are they made-up stories with a meaning?

People have all kinds of opinions about this, from those on the one hand who do not believe that God ever interferes with nature in this way, to those who feel that their faith in Jesus depends on everything in the gospel having happened just as it says.

The line taken in this book is as follows.

The memory of Jesus as a wonder-worker was so strong in the early Church (where it was sometimes felt as an embarrassment) that there must have been happenings in his life which would be described today as extraordinary or miraculous. In general, Mark's gospel reads more like an eye-witness account than does, for example, John's gospel, which is more concerned with ideas. There are many little details in Mark's gospel which have led people to think that Mark drew on the memories of Peter, who had been there with Jesus and who was later in Rome. (One example is the little detail about Jesus sleeping *on the cushion* (4:38). A leather cushion was often carried under the back seat of a fishing boat for the convenience of a passenger.) On the other hand it is often clear that the way Mark tells a particular story is governed by the Good News he wants to convey. This means that we cannot say of any particular gospel incident: 'Yes, it really happened just like that.'

But what Mark does say very clearly is that whether a particular incident happened just that way or not is *not the question*. Jesus, says Mark, never wanted to force anyone's faith by doing miracles; rather, faith was generally necessary before someone could be healed. The woman with the haemorrhage, for example, first had faith (and reached out in faith to touch his cloak) and then was made whole. Jesus said to her: *My daughter, your faith has made you well*.

Moreover, Jesus is shown in Mark's gospel as always careful not to be thought of as a wonder-worker; time and time again he forbids people to speak about the cures they have received (see p. 39). We have to remember too what chapter 1 said about a gospel, how it is not a biography, the biography of someone who is dead, but a statement about Christ living now by his spirit in the life of the believer. The experience of Mark, and of the early Church, was that faith in Jesus came by accepting to live in his way, by accepting the authority of his person and his teaching in their own lives, not by seeing marvels which could have other explanations.

The last six verses of this section (6:1–6) support this view. The people of Jesus's *own country* (Nazareth) cannot believe that the boy they had seen grow up, the man they had seen making and mending furniture and farm implements among them, could be a prophet of God. Jesus does not dazzle them with miracles to make them believe. On the contrary, because there is no encounter of faith, he cannot be a saviour for them. This section ends like the previous one. Jesus is rejected, but this time by his own people.

How do you react to the statement 'we cannot really say about any particular gospel incident: Yes, it really happened just like that'?

Make a list of all the words and phrases in 3:7 – 6:6 which refer to large numbers of people. For each give chapter and verse.
    Then make a list of all the words and phrases from the same section which suggest a small group (chapter and verse as usual).
    Look at these two lists. What kind of picture is emerging? What is Mark saying about Jesus's teaching and the response to him as a person?

# 5 Call and response: who is he?
(Mark 6:7 – 8:30)

Mark begins the next section with a 'sending-out' (mission) of the twelve apostles. What Jesus has been doing, they are to do. Note the words and phrases which identify their mission with that of Jesus. They too were to have authority over unclean spirits; they too were to preach that man should repent; they too were to cast out demons and heal the sick.

> Look up 2:32–9 and compare it with 6:7–13. In your notebook make two columns, one headed 'Jesus', the other 'the apostles.' Note down in each column, in face of each other, the phrases which you find (more or less) in both.
>     What detail concerning healing occurs in the second passage and not in the first? What practice in the early Church does it reflect? (Look up the Letter of James 5:13–15). Do any Christian churches have a similar practice today?

## John the Baptist

The fame of Jesus spreads, and the question *Who is he*? is raised. Is he a prophet? Is he Elijah, who was expected to return and herald the Messiah? Is he – as the guilty fears of Herod suggest – a reincarnation of John the Baptist? And Mark breaks off his narrative to bring his readers up-to-date with the fate of John the Baptist.

> The historical background is complicated by the marital adventures of the Herods.
>     Herod the Great (King of Judaea 37–34 BC) had married five times. By his second wife he had two sons, Aristobulus and Alexander, and Aristobulus in his turn had had two sons and a daughter. The daughter was Herodias.
>     Meanwhile by his third wife Herod the Great had had another son, Herod Philip, who had married his niece Herodias. They had a daughter, who according to the Jewish historian Josephus was called Salome.
>     And by his fourth wife Herod the Great had had yet another son, Herod Antipas – the Herod of Mark's gospel – who had become king of Judaea on his father's death. Antipas had married a princess from Nabatea, a neighbouring kingdom.
>     At the time Mark is referring to, Herod Antipas had sent away his wife and persuaded Herodias to leave her husband and come to live with him. By this action he had both snapped his fingers at the Jewish

(cont'd)

law and infuriated the Nabateans, whose princess he had insulted.

John rebuked Herod for breaking the law. He spoke as a prophet. Josephus suggests that Herod had a political motive for suppressing John: for John's denunciation of Herod's adultery could have encouraged the Nabateans to avenge their princess by invading Herod's territory.

The main facts of Mark's account agree with the main facts in Josephus, though Mark has a few minor historical inaccuracies. Mark's source was probably in the popular memories of this sensational event (court scandal!) as it was retold by the people living around. Historical details mean less to Mark than the main point.

What is the main point of the story for Mark? At first sight it looks like a digression, but Mark does not generally digress. If this is how John the Baptist finished up, he suggests, where is Jesus going?

### The feeding of the five thousand

The various incidents and stories gathered in 6:30–8:21 cluster round a central theme: that of bread. First comes the great picnic in the desert, the feeding of the five thousand (6:30–44). All four gospel-writers tell this story in some detail, and it is the only miracle-story they all have in common.

Details of the story ring true. The *blessing of the loaves* recalls the Jewish 'grace before meals', the prayer generally said over bread at the beginning of a meal. Because of the great reverence due to bread as the symbol of God's creative action in giving and sustaining life, the Jewish code of manners said that any pieces which might have fallen to the ground during a meal should be carefully collected at the end of the main course. The *baskets* were the little round baskets which the Jews normally carried with them (rather as a woman carries her handbag today). The *green grass* may sound odd in a desert place, but this was not sandy desert like the Sahara, and there were green patches (especially in the late spring) where sheep were pastured.

## Bread-echoes

The memory of this event in Jesus's life was very precious to the early Christian Church. It was lit up for them and given deeper meaning by the memory of two other bread-happenings, one which had taken place centuries before, the other which was to take place a few months later.

First, centuries before. This story in Mark is set in the desert. The phrase *a lonely place* occurs three times in verses 30–36, and the Greek word here translated *a lonely place* means *a desert*.

Now the greatest experience in the history of the Jews had been when they were set free from the slavery in Egypt and wandered forty years in the desert on their way under Moses to the Promised Land. As they went through the desert they felt God's love and protection specially shown in the mysterious food which was so unexpectedly provided for them. It covered the ground every morning as the dew dried, and they called it *manna*, which means *what is it?* The Book of Numbers tells us that it tasted *like coriander seed ... and they ground it in mills and beat it in mortars, and boiled it in pots and made cakes of it* (Num. 11:7–8). But because it was their main food during those years in the desert, they remembered it as bread, the

bread that God had fed them with in the desert as a sign of his saving love. They never forgot it. They celebrated it throughout the centuries in their prayers and hymns, and still do to this day. Mark could not speak of Jesus feeding them with bread in the desert without bringing this other bread-happening to their minds.

Secondly, for the Christian of the early Church there were other echoes. Every year the Jews celebrate the event of their going-out-of-Egypt in a Passover meal, during which they bless and share unleavened bread. In chapter 14 of his gospel Mark will tell his readers that, on the Passover before he suffered, Jesus celebrated his last meal with his apostles, and *as they were eating he took bread, and blessed and broke it, and gave it to them and said: Take, this is my body.* After his resurrection those who believed in him continued this *breaking of bread* as a living-over-again of the Last Supper, so that in this sign they might be constantly united to him in his love, his suffering and his victory over death. By the time Mark wrote this description of the feeding of the five thousand the miracle had come to be understood not only as recalling the goodness of God in the Old Testament, but also as foreshadowing Jesus's gift of himself in the Christian eucharist.

The first readers of Mark's gospel were bound to pick up these echoes. But they are not strongly underlined by Mark, as they will be later by John, and it does not seem as though the story is included here for their sake alone.

Yet Mark's emphasis on *a lonely place* suggests that he certainly wanted his readers to remember the manna. Did he want to remind them

> that **Moses**, who led the people of God through the desert, was called **shepherd and teacher**;
> that the **prophet Elisha** fed a hundred men with a few barley loaves in time of famine (2 Kings 4:42–4);
> that the **Lord** is the true **shepherd** of Israel and the manna is the **bread** that he gave?

And if this is what Mark wanted, is he in fact, through this story, asking again the question *Who is Jesus?* – the question which was hinted at in 6:14–15 and will be asked again clearly at the end of this section in 8:27–30?

It is estimated that 30% of the total population of the world do not have enough to eat, and that many thousands of men, women and children are literally starving. Do you know whether anything is being done about this?

The following ways of tackling the problem have been suggested: (a) reduce the number of people on earth; (b) increase the amount of food we produce; (c) share out more equally what is produced. Which do you think

(cont'd)

is the best solution? (You may need to do some research so that your opinion may be an informed one.)

Some people think that what actually took place in the feeding of the five thousand was a miracle of sharing – that some people had picnics in their baskets and shared them out when Jesus started it off. What do you think of this idea? Would it, in your opinion, be a lesser or a bigger miracle?

## Jesus walks on the waters

To the question: *Who is he*? Mark gives no simple and obvious answer. Instead, the question is asked once again through the mysterious story of Jesus walking on the waters (6:45–52).

Here too the clues are in the Old Testament echoes. In Psalm 77 the poet remembers how the Lord led his people out of Egypt:

> The way was through the sea,
> thy path through the great waters;
> yet thy footsteps were unseen . . .
> thou didst lead thy people like a flock. (Ps. 77:19)

And there is a strong echo from the Book of Job, from a passage which celebrates God as creator:

> Who alone stretched out the heavens,
> and trampled the waves of the sea . . .
> Lo, he passes me by and I see him not,
> he moves on, but I do not perceive him. (Job 9:8–11)

At the end of the story, when Jesus's presence has brought calm and reassurance, Mark tells us that *they were utterly and completely dumbfounded, because they had not seen what the miracle of the loaves meant.* The reference to the miracle of the loaves is understandable if behind this story too (as the Old Testament echoes suggest) lies the question *Who is he*? (Remember that the previous time Jesus was shown as having power over the sea, in 4:41, Mark says: *They were filled with awe and said one to another: Who then is this*?

To summarise. The people said:
'It is Elijah . . .';
'It is a prophet . . .';
'It is John the Baptist risen . . .'.
Like Moses, he teaches and cares for the people in the wilderness . . . as did the Lord.
Like Moses, he makes a path through the waters . . . tramples the waves of the sea . . . and passes mysteriously by . . . as did the Lord.
Like Elisha, he feeds many with a few loaves, and gives bread in the desert . . . as did the Lord.

## Who then is he?

It is as though a great insight into who he is again and again is on the point of breaking through, but they cannot perceive it, because *their minds are closed.* Remember it is part of Mark's message that they could not yet perceive it, because he was not yet risen from the dead. In the light of the resurrection and the gift of the Spirit all will be made clear.

The Christians of Rome for whom Mark was writing had known the Risen Christ, and would have their own answer to the question

*Who is he?* This last story in particular would be full of meaning and comfort for them (as for many Christians since) in the storm of persecution which raged around them.

## At table together (7:1 – 8:10)
Still following the theme of bread, the four units which compose 7:1 – 8:10 form a sequence, together conveying one central message. The units are:

an argument with the scribes and Pharisees concerning
ritual observance (7:1–23)
the story of the Syro-Phoenician woman (7:24–30)
the healing of the deaf-and-dumb man (7:31–37) and
the feeding of the four thousand (8:1–10).

To understand why these four episodes are linked, and to grasp their message, it is necessary to recall one great problem in the life of the early Christian Church.

Quite soon after the resurrection both the apostle Peter and the apostle Paul received gentiles (i.e. non-Jews) into the Christian community. They did this independently of one another, but in response to what they believed to be clear guidance from the Holy Spirit. When this was noticed, it was challenged by many of the Jewish converts. Their point of view was that Jesus had been a Jew, a descendant of the great King David, and that in his person the promises which God had made to his people were fulfilled. For them, Christianity did not mean a break with the Jewish religion, but a purified form of it and its fulfilment. And so they thought that if non-Jews wanted to follow Jesus, they should first of all accept to be circumcised as Jews and undertake to keep all the prescriptions of the Jewish law.

Others had a much broader view of who Jesus was and who he had come for. They believed that his coming and his teaching represented something really new, a breakthrough of God's spirit into the world; and that all men were called to follow him, no matter whether they were Jews or not. In The Acts of the Apostles, chapter 15, Peter has an experience which leads him to declare: *God does not have favourites, but anybody of any nationality who fears God and does what is right is acceptable to him*. And Paul, writing to the Christians of Rome, maintains that Jewish law has been replaced by *the law of the spirit of life in Christ Jesus* (Romans 8:2). *For the kingdom of God is not food and drink but righteousness and peace and joy in the Holy Spirit*.

On both sides feelings were strong, and it looked as though the argument would divide the Christian community. So its leaders called a big meeting in Jerusalem in the year AD 49. At that meeting the case for both sides was put. Peter and Paul explained why they had done what they had done, and all were allowed to put their point of view. Finally a decision was arrived at: gentiles were not to be obliged to become Jews before becoming Christians, but gentile converts were asked to be considerate of the feelings of their ex-Jewish fellow-believers, and not to eat the meat of animals killed in certain ways which the Jews considered unfit.

This meeting, generally known as the first *Council of Jerusalem*, settled the question once and for all. (You can read all about it, and the events which led up to it, in The Acts of the Apostles, chapters 10 and 15.) But it was one thing to decide on a principle, and another to live out its practical consequences. It was especially difficult when Jewish-Christians and gentile-Christians met at the Eucharist and at the meal which followed it. The Jewish-Christians had been brought up to follow very strict laws about food ... about what should be eaten, how it should be cooked and what were the appropriate table-manners. They could hardly help being disgusted by the manners of their gentile-Christian companions. Some of them even felt that gentiles, if they could become Christians, should not be admitted to the Eucharist. So anything in the gospel which could throw light on this problem would be of great interest especially to the Christians of Rome, who as gentile converts might find themselves in danger of being discriminated against.

### Argument with the scribes and Pharisees (7:1–23)

Mark next shows Jesus arguing with a group of scribes and Pharisees about the laws of ceremonial washing which pious Jews observed before eating a meal. Jesus passes no judgement on the laws themselves, but goes more deeply into the matter by pointing out that mere outward keeping of any law does not make a man holy, since holiness comes from the heart. He reminds his hearers that Isaiah had condemned the people of his day for thinking that true religion consists in mere outward observance; and he gives an example to show how blindness on this point can lead one to put man-made laws before even the most fundamental obligations of justice.

This example (see 7:9–13) refers to a practice under Jewish traditional law whereby anything set apart for the service of God cannot be claimed for any other purpose. The formula for dedicating to God (the *Corban* formula) had come to be used very frequently, even when there was no intention of actually handing over to the service of the temple what you had 'corbaned'. And if you said that all you possessed was 'corbaned' you could even get away with not helping your parents when they were in need. Which, as Jesus pointed out, was against God's commandment to honour one's father and mother.

Jesus in this was not criticising the laws themselves, but he was criticising *legalism*, that is, thinking that as long as you keep the law you are all right. Jesus is opposed to such a spirit; he maintains that it is the interior disposition of a man or woman, what they have in their hearts, that makes them good or evil. But his hearers do not seem to be able to get away from their obsession with unclean food. Jesus works really hard: first he tries to convince the scribes and Pharisees; then he repeats the lesson to *the people* (v. 14), and finally to *the disciples* – with the help of a mini-biology-lesson to remind them that the body has its own way of getting rid of the unwanted parts of food! But what truly defiles a man are the wicked thoughts and intentions in his heart. In verse 19 Mark applies the lesson directly to the particular food-problems of the early Church.

Why do you think it was so difficult for Jesus's hearers to understand what he was saying here? Think yourself especially into the shoes of the scribes and Pharisees: why might they consider Jesus's teaching even. dangerous?

Have you found in your own experience, or in what you have read in newspapers, examples of 'legalism' – which does not mean concern for law (which society needs) but paying more attention to keeping the law than to intentions?

Outward deeds are more easy to assess and to measure than are intentions. Do you think this is a problem for those whom society appoints to guard the law? What is the difference in law between murder and manslaughter? What is the definition in law of theft?

### The Syro-Phoenician woman (7:24–30)
The next episode begins abruptly. *And from there he arose and went away to the region of Tyre and Sidon.* Mark is not really changing the subject, however, but continuing it.

Tyre and Sidon were international seaports on the Mediterranean coast (see map on p. 38). Not only were they in pagan country, but like most international ports they had a bad reputation. From the way Jesus refers to them in Matthew 11:21 it would seem that they had become a byword for pagan wickedness. The woman who comes to him there is a *Greek*, (i.e. a non-Jew), *a Syro-Phoenician by birth*. Mark is emphasising that she is a gentile both by birth and by upbringing.

The answer Jesus gives to her prayer pulls the reader up short by its harshness. *Gentile dogs* was a term of contempt sometimes used by the Jews, whose conviction that they were God's chosen people could make them racial snobs. True, the word used by Jesus was the word for a puppy-dog, a family pet rather than the wilder and fiercer dog that roamed the streets. But it was still a snub, and it arrests the attention of the reader and underlines still further the fact that the woman was a gentile. She, however, sparkles back with a witty reply, and Jesus, seeing what disposition of the heart lay behind her answer, gives her what she asks.

As often in Mark, this vivid miracle-story holds the clue to the whole teaching sequence. Jesus has tried without success to convince the Pharisees that what makes a man a member of God's household is not the keeping of traditional pious practices, but the disposition of the heart. He has repeated the lesson to the crowd with no greater success, and the disciples do not seem to have understood him any better. So in Mark's account he gets up, treks some sixty miles north-west into the heart of pagan country, meets a woman who knows nothing of the traditions of the ancients, and perceives that, because of the disposition of heart with which she meets him, she too can receive the salvation that comes from him.

### The healing of a deaf and dumb man (7:31–37)

If there is any confusion still about what Mark is trying to say, what follows will make it clear. Jesus now travels on north to Sidon, then round towards the sea of Galilee through *the region of the ten towns* (*Decapolis*). That is, he remains in pagan country. There he cures a man who is deaf and dumb.

The story is told vividly. Jesus's actions are described, his use of spittle (which was thought to have curative properties) and the very Aramaic word he used. But the real meaning of the miracle story as placed by Mark in this context is shown by the last sentence: *He has done all things well; he even makes the deaf hear and the dumb speak.*

Again the reader is meant to catch the echoes. One of the best-loved passages of the Old Testament was a beautiful poem in the Book of Isaiah in which the prophet sings of the signs which will accompany the salvation God is preparing for his people:

> Then the eyes of the blind shall be opened,
>   and the ears of the deaf unstopped;
> then shall the lame man leap like a hart,
>   and the tongue of the dumb sing for joy.
>                                       (Isaiah 35:5)

It has happened, says Mark, and it has happened among the pagans. Through Jesus salvation has come to everyone.

### The feeding of the four thousand (8:1–9)

And Mark goes on to show a final expression of this gift to the gentiles. In 8:1–9 he tells of another *feeding in the wilderness*, this time of four thousand men. The story is told only in its bare essentials. It is useless to waste time arguing whether there were indeed two different 'feedings', or whether Mark has used two different folk-memories of the one event. By placing this story here Mark completes his statement about gentiles being admitted to full Christian fellowship. (Note that there are no longer twelve baskets left, but seven ... a number which among the Jews suggested fullness or infinity.) Having met a gentile woman and given her salvation, having worked among the gentiles the accepted sign of the coming of the kingdom of God, Jesus now distributes to the gentiles also, in abundance, the bread of the children. What Jew-Christian, after reading this, would dare to suggest that the Christian convert from paganism ought not to be admitted to the Eucharist?

Whether these stories were already linked in the teaching of the early Church, or whether it was Mark who linked them in this way, we cannot know for sure. But the style of the joining-up verses suggests to scholars that it was Mark's arrangement. If so, then he was indeed threading his beads (see chapter 2) to make his statement powerful and clear.

## Sign from heaven

This sequence completed, Mark picks up again the theme: *Who is he?* The Pharisees are hostile. They ask him to prove in some way that he is a prophet from God; otherwise they will kill him as a false prophet according to the law (Deut. 13:2–6). But miracles are not for proving. The phrase *seeking . . . to test him* shows that they were hostile, and Jesus, recognising a disposition of the heart which closes them to an understanding of his message, refuses.

In the incident which follows (8:14–21) the *leaven* (or yeast) of the Pharisees and of Herod stands for their spirit of unbelief and hostility which can contaminate even those who follow him more closely. The disciples are shown as utterly confused; they cannot really follow what is going on; they cannot perceive who he is.

### The blind man of Bethsaida (8:22–6)

Sometimes it takes time to learn to see. The cure of the blind man of Bethsaida is the only gradual cure in the gospel. Finally, however, he looks intently and is restored, and sees clearly.

## Peter's statement of faith (8:27–30)

So, finally, do the apostles – or so it seems. The question *Who is he?* is taken up again, this time explicitly raised by Jesus himself (v. 27). The various answers which have been hinted at in this section are again listed: John the Baptist? Elijah? One of the prophets?

And then Peter sees. *You are the Christ.* (Christ = Messiah = anointed One: the term used for the Deliverer, and the title given consistently to Jesus by the Christians after the resurrection.) This confession of faith by Peter is the climax to which the whole of this section has been leading. It can be seen as the turning point of Mark's gospel.

# 6 The cost of discipleship
## (Mk 8:31 – 10:52)

It was one thing to say: *You are the Christ*, another thing to know what these words implied. Mark spends much of his next section correcting false ideas about the Messiah.

The Jews at the time of Jesus were expecting a Messiah, whom many thought would be a freedom-fighter sent by God to free them from Roman power. There is evidence in the gospels and elsewhere that people soon began to think of Jesus in this way: and Mark shows that even the apostles did so. From 8:31 onwards he shows Jesus trying to correct false ideas about his Messiahship, forecasting that his preaching would not lead to a political or military victory. On the contrary, it would lead to a clash with the authorities in which he would be the loser. Moreover, those who followed him were to expect the same for themselves. And in forecasting this, Jesus teaches a great deal too about the values of the 'kingdom' he has come to establish, not at all the kind of kingdom they were expecting.

There may have been another reason why Mark feels the need to emphasise this. In the Near-Eastern countries into which Christianity had spread, there existed a popular cult of magicians, of wonder-workers, who were very much looked up to, and even called *divine men* because of the powers they displayed. (We have already seen Mark's anxiety that Jesus should not be put into this category: see p. 40.) Something of this cult may have rubbed off on to the Christians, so that those among them who for example had the gift of healing would find themselves regarded as very special people. There is a theory, based mainly on Paul's second letter to the Corinthians, that in the troubled state of a persecuted Church, such people were sometimes carried away by the sense of power which the gift of healing gave them, and even went so far as to proclaim themselves second Christs, or *Christ come again*. To them and to those who believed them Mark gives the stern warning: the *good news of Jesus Christ* is not that all suffering is over and the day of triumph at hand, but that the way of final happiness is the way of continued suffering and humiliation, for the Christian as well as for Jesus himself. This is the reality of Christian discipleship which Mark's first readers were experiencing in their own lives; and they were to look for salvation, says Mark, there and nowhere else.

Mark is really doing two things at once in this section. In showing how Jesus took care to correct false ideas of his Messiahship which were in the minds of the apostles and other people of his day, Mark warns the first-century Christians against the same kind of mistake, and helps them to understand better what being a follower of Jesus is really about.

So Jesus begins to talk about the sufferings and death which lie ahead of him. Three times he foretells the way his life will end: in 8:31, in 9:31 and in 10:33,34.

> Look up these passages. Compare them. What details are included each time?
>
> Some people understand from these passages that Jesus was really able to foresee the future, by a special power which belonged to him as a totally exceptional individual. Others think he simply realised that he was on a collision course with the authorities, and knew that, because violent resistance was against the law of love which governed his life, the whole adventure would end in his death. And this is what he talked about. The details of his sufferings and death would then have been filled in by Mark with hindsight, to strengthen the dramatic effect. What do you think?
>
> Do you know of any men or women in this century who have lost their lives (or are likely to do so) because of their concern for their fellow human beings, or their loyalty to their conscience?

The context of these 'foretellings' is important. The first (8:31) comes immediately after Peter's confession of faith. It shows straight away that although Peter might say *You are the Christ*, he did not really understand what it meant. In fact, Peter's understanding was so different from that of Jesus that it put them on opposite sides, so to speak, in Jesus's struggle against evil.

The second 'foretelling' (9:31) comes immediately after the Trans-figuration and the cure of the epileptic boy, as though Jesus was afraid that these two happenings might encourage them in their mistaken ideas. He did not have much success. Mark says: *They did not understand the saying, and they were afraid to ask him* (9:32).

The third is the most detailed (10:33,34). This time the apostles do not even seem to have heard what was said, because the next moment they are arguing about who is to have the highest place in his kingdom (10:34,35).

The impression we get throughout this section is that the followers of Jesus are less and less able to follow what he is saying, or to understand the meaning of what he is doing. They cannot keep up with him even physically.

> Note all the places in 8:31–10:45 where it says that Jesus's disciples did not understand what he was saying.
>
> Then look up 9:33, 10:23, 10:32 and 10:35. What do these verses suggest about the way Jesus and his disciples walked along the road to Jerusalem?

## Followers on the way

Mark goes even further. To each of these 'foretellings' he attaches a teaching of Jesus which emphasises still more what being a follower of Jesus really means, and how different it is from what they were expecting.

Like most people, the disciples were concerned with their future well-being, which in their case was bound up with Jesus's victory. But in 8:34–8 Jesus says, not only that he will die, but that those who would be his followers must be prepared to give up all they have, even their lives if necessary, for his way of love. (The expression *take up his cross* would be clearly understood by his listeners: crucifixion was the official form of execution, under Roman law, for those – like the Jews – who were not Roman citizens.) And in a paradox (i.e. an apparent contradiction) he expresses one of the basic truths about human living.

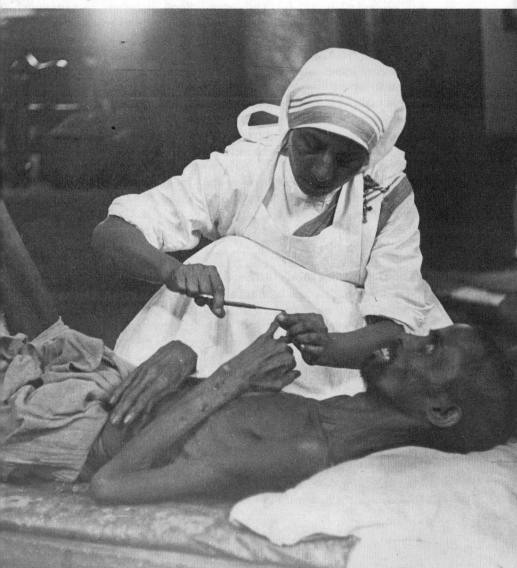

Think about the words of Jesus: *Whoever would save his life will lose it; and whoever loses his life for my sake and for the gospel will save it.*
What do you think these words mean? Do you know anyone (in real life or in literature) in whose life they are seen clearly to be true?

After the second prediction, Jesus gives a lesson about his understanding of authority as the service of others (9:33–5). The apostles had been discussing *who was the greatest*: and Jesus *called them* (for an official teaching, that is, not a casual remark) and said: *If anyone would be first, he must be the least of all.*

And after the third prediction, Jesus gives yet another lesson to his followers. The lesson is contained within an amusing little incident which shows how little they had understood so far. James and John, still apparently expecting that Jesus would soon lead a successful rebellion, ask for the first and second places in the government which they thought he would set up. Jesus asks instead whether they are prepared to follow him on the way of suffering, which he refers to as being baptised with a special baptism and drinking from a special cup. And James and John are not the only ones who have the wrong idea; so have the other apostles. They are angry with James and John, presumably for stealing a march on the rest and getting in first with their request for the best jobs. Jesus in reply emphasises how different are the values of his kingdom from those of men in general: just as he has come not to be served but to serve, to the extent of giving his life for mankind, so among his followers *whoever would be great among you must be your servant.* Ever since Mark's gospel was written, the words of Jesus in 8:34–5 and 10:42–5 have expressed something of the deepest meaning of being a Christian. The truth they express is at the heart of Mark's message.

### The rich young man (10:17–31)
The story of the rich young man, with its sequel in 10:23–31, is another expression of how the call to follow Jesus demands total giving of oneself. The story is vividly told, with the kind of detail that makes the reader feel he is watching it happen. The man *ran up ... he knelt ... his face fell ... he went away sorrowing ...* Jesus *looked upon him ... loved him.* Unlike other occasions when questions are put to Jesus, there is no suggestion of a trap; the young man seems sincere. As the conversation proceeds Jesus finally invites him to discipleship (*follow me*), which for this young man meant freeing himself from slavery to possessions. His failure to respond leads on to Jesus's teaching on the difficulty (or impossibility) of having riches without their becoming an obstacle to the unselfish gift of oneself for the kingdom. Jesus's words are strong. The expression *it is easier for a camel to pass through the eye of a needle than for a rich man to enter the*

*kingdom of heaven* is so uncomfortable to listen to that people have tried to weaken it, by suggesting that *camel* is a misreading for *rope* (the two words are very similar in Greek), or that *needle* really refers to a gate into Jerusalem so low that camels had to go through it on their knees. But similar expressions have been found in the literature of the time, where an *elephant passing through the eye of a needle* is clearly a metaphorical way of saying that something is impossible; and that is what Jesus is saying here. The disciples are amazed because in Jewish thought, as we see from the Old Testament, riches were generally thought of as a sign of God's blessing. So Jesus's teaching, his attitude towards the rich whom he seems rather to pity than to envy or condemn, would be puzzling to his hearers. Peter's subsequent question and the answer Jesus gives complete the paradox and make the whole story a particular illustration of 8:35.

Do you know what is meant by the expression *consumer society*? Get an elderly person to help you make a list of all the things in your living room at home which would not have been there fifty years ago. Do you think we are necessarily happier because we have so many things around us?

Have you ever experienced (a) being really miserable because you lacked something which was absolutely necessary to your well-being? (b) living for a while in a very simple, even rough way, and enjoying it?

What do you think about riches and poverty in today's world?

## Marriage and divorce (10:1–13)

Maybe Jesus's teaching on divorce fits into the same line of development, since it is also very demanding. It is recorded by Mark as an *argument* story. The question is asked *in order to test him*.

Most of the Jews agreed that divorce was permitted, though they argued about the grounds for divorce. Their opinion was based on a passage in Deuteronomy 24:1–4, where there is legislation for a woman who has been divorced. The purpose of the law was to protect the woman, so that the husband who *writes out a bill of divorce and puts it into her hand and sends her out of his house* (it sounds as though she had no say in it at all) may not reclaim her later if he changes his mind, but must respect the freedom he has given her. This is the text the Pharisees are referring to. Jesus's reply is clear: in affirming that marriage is indissoluble he goes beyond what is to what should be, by appealing to the plan of God as shown in creation.

> Statistics suggest that one marriage in three today is likely to end in divorce. What do you think are the reasons for the great increase in the rate of divorce during the last twenty years?

## Little children

One of the best-known passages in this section is 10:13–16. It is generally agreed that we have here the memory of an event in Jesus's life which shows an attitude towards children, a respect and a

tenderness, unusual in the society to which he belonged. At the same time it is more than a pretty story; the conflict between Jesus and his disciples is thrown into strong relief by the words Mark uses to describe it (*rebuked* ... *was indignant*) and leads on to a lesson in the attitude required of a Christian.

Try to describe in your own words the Christian way of life, as Jesus has talked about it in these passages from Mark's gospel. Do you think it is an impossible ideal?

In the course of history there have been people who have followed Jesus's teaching to a heroic degree. The Christian Church recognises and honours such people. Choose someone who you think has lived the ideals of Christianity to an extraordinary degree. Read up his or her life and be prepared to talk about it to your class.

## The Transfiguration (9:2–13)

In these ways Mark corrects false ideas of Jesus's Messiahship by showing what it will mean for Jesus and what it asks of his followers. At the same time there is no doubt in Mark's mind that he *is* the Messiah. Sandwiched effectively between the first and second prediction of the passion comes what we call the *Transfiguration*. In this event, mysterious and full of symbolic detail, the faith of Peter, James and John is made stronger by a 'flash-forward', an anticipation, of Jesus's final glory.

Once again, there are many echoes we need to catch, many clues to meaning. The most important are:

*Moses and Elijah*: These are the two leading figures of the Old Testament, one representing law and the other prophecy.

*The mountain*: It was on a mountain that, after six days of waiting, Moses met the glory of the Lord and was so transfigured that when he came down again *the skin of his face shone ... and they were afraid to come near him* (Exodus 24:5–16 and 34:29)

*The cloud*: Throughout the Old Testament a cloud is the sign of God's presence: in the Tent of Meeting, for example, and in the journey through the desert (see Exodus, chapter 40) and in the temple (1 Kings 8:10, 11).

*Three tents*: When God is spoken of as 'dwelling' among his people, the word used means literally 'pitching his tent'. The words *tent*, *tabernacle* and *booth* all mean the same thing. Zechariah, in his vision of the End-time, speaks of the Lord coming and pitching his tent once more among men (Zech. 2:10).

*Garments glistening ... intensely white*: In the centuries immediately before the birth of Jesus the Jews dreamed of the End-time as the day when all injustice would be destroyed and righteousness restored. There is a famous passage in the Second Book of Maccabees, a book written in the second century BC to describe the struggle of the Jewish resistance movement against a foreign conqueror. The writer looks forward to the day of final victory when *God gathers his people together again and shows them his mercy ... and the Lord will bring these things once more to light, and the glory of the Lord will be seen, and so will the cloud, as it was revealed in the time of Moses.* (2 Macc. 2:8). But the most famous vision of the End-time was that of the seventh chapter of the Book of Daniel:

> As I looked
> thrones were placed
> and one that was ancient of days took his seat.
> His raiment was white as snow ...
> and behold, with the clouds of heaven
> there came one like a son of man,
> and he came to the ancient of days
> and was presented before him
> and to him was given dominion
> and glory and kingdom,
> that all peoples, nations and languages
> should serve him;
> his dominion is an everlasting dominion
> which shall not pass away,
> and his kingdom one
> that shall not be destroyed.
>
> (Daniel 7:9 and 13–14)

There are other references too, but these are the most important. To trace their echoes in Mark's account of the Transfiguration is to discover great richness of meaning. For Mark it affirms strongly the faith, both of the apostles and of his readers, in the Messiahship of Jesus. Mark spends so much time in this section correcting false ideas about Jesus, but he leaves his readers in no doubt that Peter's insight in 8:30 was truer than he knew, and that Jesus is, as the title of Mark's gospel proclaimed, *Christ the Son of God*.

How would you describe, in your own words, what you think was the experience of the Apostles on the mountain of Transfiguration?
  How does Mark say symbolically in this passage
  (a) that Jesus is the fulfilment of all the past history of his people;
  (b) that he represents a special presence of God among men;
  (c) that somehow in his destiny the perfect reign of God will be achieved?

For the rest, this section contains two miracle stories and a little collection of miscellaneous sayings which seem to be linked together by the *catch-word* method (see p. 22).

The sayings are contained in 9:36–50. Jesus had said that he who wants to be first must be *servant* of all. The Aramaic word for *servant* is the same as *child*, and that may have reminded Mark again of Jesus's love for children, and led him on to record the saying *Whoever receives a child in my name receives me*. *In my name* recalls the problem of the man who was casting out demons in *Jesus's name*, and whom the apostles had rebuked because he was not one of them. Jesus reproaches them for their narrowness. The same phrase is a link with the next saying ... and so it continues through the link words *little one ... cause to sin ... fire ... salt ...* to the end of verse 50.

A few background notes help to make these sayings clearer to the modern reader.

To be thrown into the sea with a stone tied round one's neck was a Roman form of punishment, though not unknown to the Jews. The *great mill-stone* is literally a *donkey-stone*, that is, one turned by a donkey as distinct from the lighter hand-mill turned by women.

*Hell* in verse 43 is literally *Gehenna*, the valley south of Jerusalem. To the Jews it was an abominable place because it had been in the past the place where babies were burned in sacrifice to the pagan god Moloch. In Jesus's time it served as a rubbish dump for the city, where offal would be maggoty and fires burned day and night to destroy the city's refuse.

*Salted with fire* is a strange expression: perhaps it refers to ancient medical practice, where both the application of salt and cauterisation were used to prevent wounds from turning septic. Another suggestion is that both salt and fire suggest a process of purification, and even today *passing through fire* is an image for having to undergo great suffering, such as persecution.

Salt cannot really *lose its savour*, but the salty deposits around the Dead Sea keep the white appearance of salt even when the saltness has been washed away by the rain.

All these references to the contemporary background suggest that these sayings go back to Jesus himself. Linking them together through catch-words helped people to remember them, and they were probably already so linked before Mark took them up and put them into his gospel here.

Try to express in your own words the teaching found in the sentences beginning:
(a) If anyone would be first . . .
(b) Whoever gives you a cup of cold water . . .
(c) Whoever causes one of these little ones to sin . . .
(d) If your hand causes you to sin . . .
(e) Salt is good, but if . . .

### Miracle stories (9:14–29 and 10:46–52)

The two miracle stories in this section are the healing of the *boy with a dumb spirit* (or the epileptic boy) and the healing of *blind Bartimaeus*. Both are full of vivid detail.

The first emphasises the need for at least a beginning of faith, and fits well into the main theme of this section. It underlines that the power to heal is not something which a disciple of Jesus possesses and can 'turn on' at will. It may have served as a useful warning to the more confident miracle-workers among the Christians of Mark's day (see p. 63).

The story of the healing of blind Bartimaeus seems to have been included here because of its connection with Jericho. The title he gives to Jesus (Son of David) is new in Mark's gospel, and has a particular appropriateness as Jesus approaches Jerusalem, the city founded by David, of whose descendants the Messiah was expected to be born.

In order to bring out the main thrust of Mark's writing, this chapter has followed each strand of thought separately rather than in the order in which Mark wrote. The table shows the way in which these strands are interwoven, and gives the plan of the whole.

*Mark 8.31 – 10.52*

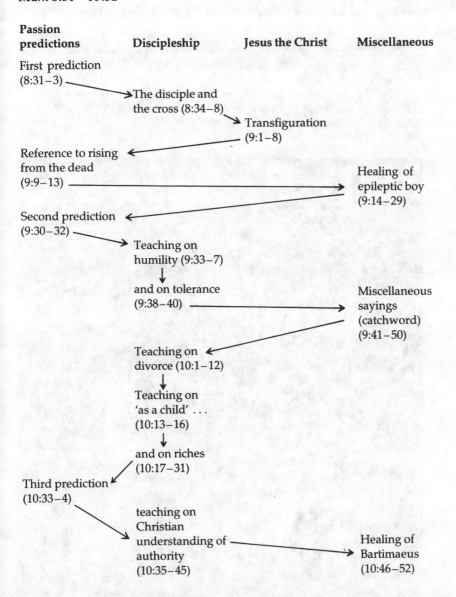

| Passion predictions | Discipleship | Jesus the Christ | Miscellaneous |
|---|---|---|---|
| First prediction (8:31–3) | The disciple and the cross (8:34–8) | Transfiguration (9:1–8) | |
| Reference to rising from the dead (9:9–13) | | | Healing of epileptic boy (9:14–29) |
| Second prediction (9:30–32) | Teaching on humility (9:33–7) and on tolerance (9:38–40) | | Miscellaneous sayings (catchword) (9:41–50) |
| | Teaching on divorce (10:1–12) Teaching on 'as a child' ... (10:13–16) and on riches (10:17–31) | | |
| Third prediction (10:33–4) | teaching on Christian understanding of authority (10:35–45) | | Healing of Bartimaeus (10:46–52) |

# 7 Jerusalem

With the arrival of Jesus in Jerusalem, Mark's narrative takes on a different character. It is full of action; events press upon one another, and lead with a kind of inevitability to the climax of the sufferings and death of Jesus. Mark's gospel has sometimes been described as the story of the sufferings and death of Jesus with an introduction.

> Look back over the ten chapters you have studied so far, and collect all the references you can find, direct or indirect, to the sufferings and the death of Jesus.
>
> Does your collection fit in with the theory that Mark was especially interested in the sufferings and death of Jesus? Why do you think that these events have such importance for him?

Three times each year all the adult Jews who could went on pilgrimage to Jerusalem to celebrate a great religious festival.

The first of these was the festival of the Passover (March–April). It was originally a feast of the springtime, a celebration of new life: unleavened bread (that is, bread without yeast) was eaten, and a lamb was sacrificed and eaten. It had become a celebration of the day when the Hebrews were freed from slavery in Egypt, and were born again as a people. But its celebration was more than an empty memory; every Jew who celebrated it with devotion felt himself again in touch with the love which had saved his forefathers. One of the prayers of the feast-day says:

'Not our ancestors only did the Holy One redeem, but us as well along with them, as it is written: And God freed us from Egypt so as to take us and give us the land sworn to our ancestors. Therefore let us rejoice at the wonder of our deliverance from bondage to freedom, from agony to joy, from mourning to festivity, from darkness to light, from servitude to redemption. Before God let us ever sing a new song.'
    (from *A Passover Haggadah*, ed. Bronstein, Penguin, 1974.)

A description of the origin of the feast is in Exodus 12:1–13,42.)

The second festival was the Feast of Weeks, the wheat-harvest festival, celebrated seven weeks (fifty days) after the Passover, and therefore called Pentecost. It commemorated the giving of the ten commandments on Mount Sinai (see Exodus, chapters 19 and 20).

The third was the harvest festival, called the Feast of Tabernacles or Tents, which fell in September or October. In thanksgiving for the fruitfulness of the earth, branches of citron, palm, myrtle and willow were carried in procession with joyful singing of psalms. Branches were used to build the tents or shacks in which the main meal was eaten. These tents recalled the protection given to the people by God during their wanderings in the desert, and also the divine shelter under which men will live when his Kingdom will be established at the end of time.

The story opens with the approach of Jesus to Jerusalem, cheered by the crowds, by *those who went before and whose who followed*. The scene fits well into the usual setting of a pilgrimage going up to Jerusalem for a great feast.

The details which help to build up the story and relate it to its setting are:

(a) *And those who went before and those who followed cried out: Hosanna! Blessed is he who comes in the name of the Lord! Blessed is the kingdom of our father David that is coming. Hosanna in the highest* (11:9–10). This is an echo of Psalm 118, one of the pilgrimage psalms sung on these occasions. *Hosanna* means *Save us, O Lord*.

(b) ... *leafy branches which they had cut from the fields* (11:8). The waving of branches is a sign of rejoicing which sometimes accompanied the singing of the psalms. In fact, so closely were these branches of greenery connected with Psalm 118 that they were sometimes called *Hosannas*.

(c) *And they brought the colt to Jesus, and ... he sat upon it* (11:7). The Greek word here translated *colt* is the same as that used by the prophet Zechariah in a famous passage which the reader is meant to recall. The prophet, describing the *day of the Lord*, sees the king coming triumphant and victorious, humble and riding on *an ass, a colt the foal of an ass* (Zechariah 9:9).

Mark emphasises the apparent detail of the colt (how many times does he mention it?). It was an unusual way to take part in a pilgrimage; normally pilgrims deliberately finished the journey on foot, whatever transport they might have used in the earlier stages of their journey.

> What do you think Mark may have been suggesting by the link he makes between Jesus and the prophet Zechariah, and between Jesus and the Messianic psalm: *Blessed is he . . .*?

The actual event, which Mark sees as so significant, would probably have been sufficiently covered up by the general excitement of a feast-day pilgrimage to have passed unperceived by most people. It does not seem to have attracted the notice of the authorities. Entering Jerusalem, Jesus then visits the temple rapidly, and *as it was already late*, goes out to Bethany (a village within easy walking distance, where according to the other gospels Jesus had friends), and spends the night there with *the twelve*.

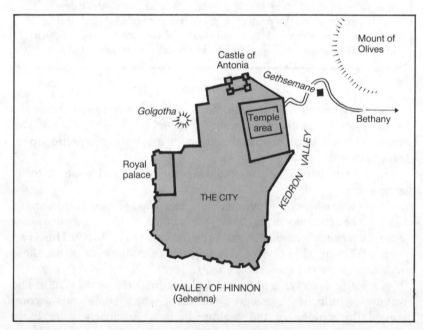

## Holy Week

The next verse begins: *On the following day* ... This is the first of a series of time-references which seem to programme the events of chapters 11–16 with unusual precision. Picked out, they suggest the following calendar:

| | | |
|---|---|---|
| **Sunday**: | | Triumphal entry into Jerusalem |
| **Monday**: | *On the following day* (11:12) | The fig-tree without figs. Jesus casts out dealers from the temple. |
| | and when evening came (11:19) | He spends the night *out of the city*: Bethany? |
| **Tuesday**: | *in the morning* (11:20) | The fig-tree withered. Jesus's authority questioned. Parable of vineyard. Three 'arguments'. |
| | Later, *as Jesus taught in the temple* (12:35) | he asks a question, condemns the scribes, and praises the women's offering. |
| | Later still, *as he came out of the temple ... and sat down on the Mount of Olives* | he prophesies the destruction of Jerusalem and the coming of the End-time. |
| **Wednesday**: | *It was two days before the Passover and the Unleavened Bread* (14:1) | Jesus was at Bethany, where a woman anointed him. His death is plotted. |
| **Thursday**: | *On the first day of the Unleavened Bread* (14:12) *When it was evening* (14:17) | Jesus eats with apostles. He leaves for Gethsemane and is arrested. |
| **Friday**: | *As soon as it was morning* | Jesus is taken to Pilate, scourged and |
| | *at the third hour* (15:25) | is crucified. After three hours |
| | *when the sixth hour had come When evening was come, since it was the day of Preparation the day before the sabbath* | he dies.<br><br>he is buried. |
| **Saturday**: | The sabbath day | |
| **Sunday**: | *when the sabbath was past very early on the first day of the week* (16:22) | the women find the grave empty. |

Mark in fact makes no link in time between the events of the *Tuesday* and those of the *Wednesday*. But if we presume a link (and the way in which it is told tempts us to do so) then all these happenings fit into one week. The victorious entry of Jesus into Jerusalem would fit into the context of the pilgrims coming up to Jerusalem for the Passover feast, and the death of Jesus would coincide with the sacrificing of the Paschal lamb and the Jewish celebration of their deliverance from Egypt and the hope of final deliverance by the Messiah. Every year the Christian Church celebrates the memory of these events during the week before Easter, which is called *Holy Week*, beginning with Palm Sunday and closing with Easter Sunday. We know that they have been so celebrated in the liturgy (that is, in the official public prayer of the Church) since the fourth century at least.

Yet there are difficulties if Mark's narrative is taken to mean that all these events actually happened during the last week of Jesus's life. An alternative theory is that they were in reality spread over the last six months of his life.

The main arguments for this are:
(a) The calendar for Tuesday and for Friday, as given above, is incredibly crowded.
(b) The picture Mark gives of Jesus's entry into Jerusalem could fit into the context of any pilgrimage entry into Jerusalem, but in fact fits most neatly into the context of the Feast of Tabernacles (Sept./Oct.). In the ceremony of this feast Psalm 118 was always chanted, and the *Hosanna* verse repeated as a chorus, with the shaking of bundles of palm, myrtle and willow branches. The Jewish liturgical reading for the Feast of Tabernacles is from the Book of Zechariah, the very prophecy which is alluded to by the mention of the colt.
(c) The story of the fig-tree which had no figs is also easier to understand if the event took place in the early autumn rather than in spring (see below, p. 79).

Those who think that we have here six months' events compressed into one week have to ask themselves why Mark does this. Does he do it consciously for literary effect, or did his sources already present them in this way? One explanation could be that, by the time he wrote, the celebration of *Holy Week* had already become common in the early Church, and that, because of this, the memory of the triumphant entry into Jerusalem had become identified with the Passover rather than with Tabernacles. Living as we do in a world where the written word is very important, we tend to think of the gospel as a word first written and then prayed. But it was not so in the culture of the time. The Jews had preserved their own history by celebrating it in prayer before ever they wrote it down, and the early Christian Church certainly did the same. We know, for example, that some passages from Paul's letters (which are earlier than the gospels) are quotations from early Christian hymns, and it would not be at all surprising to find that the writing of a gospel had been influenced by the prayer-life of the early Church.

This second theory, in any case, makes better sense of the incident which follows, the curious incident of the fig-tree which had no figs. If this happened on the Monday before the Passover (i.e. in March/April) then it was unreasonable to expect to find figs on the tree. The fig-tree loses its leaves in winter – one of the few trees in Palestine which are not evergreen. It comes into leaf in the springtime, and though some of the previous year's figs may then still be on the branches, and the first signs of the new year's fruit may have appeared, neither of these would be fit to eat. So you could not expect edible figs in the springtime. But if these events were associated with the Feast of Tabernacles, which is (among other things) a kind of harvest festival in the autumn, then it would be normal to find figs among the large leaves. Moreover, in the autumn any such tree which bore no figs would appear barren and withered when the leaves fell (compare verse 20). On the other hand, the text points out (v. 13) *that it was not the season* for figs, which brings us back to springtime and the Passover. It has been suggested that this phrase may have been slipped in later by a copyist, writing when the 'one-week' calendar had already been accepted, and suddenly thinking: 'But it wasn't the season for figs anyhow.' But we have no textual evidence for this (textual evidence means, for example, that when a copyist does put in something of his own, we generally find it included in some of the early manuscripts but not in all). So the argument goes to and fro.

Summarise the arguments for and against the theory that the events of *Holy Week* did not in fact take place within one week, but rather within six months. Which seems to you most likely?

## The fig-tree (11:12–14,20–25)

However it may be (and we cannot know for certain one way or another) the total effect of these chapters is dramatic as the tension increases. The question of the calendar is not so important. The point of the fig-tree story, for example, is lost if one pays attention only to the question of date. For it has a deeper meaning, and is rather like a parable, or like one of those striking actions which the prophets of the Old Testament used, to bring home their message. The clue to its understanding is in the Old Testament. There the fig-tree is one of the two commonest symbols of the people of God (the other being the vine). The failure of the people to be true to its calling is described by Jeremiah in words which the gospel incident is meant to recall:

> When I would gather them, says the Lord,
> there are no grapes on the vine,
> no figs on the fig-tree,
> even the leaves have withered,
> and what I gave them has passed away from them.
> (Jeremiah 8:13)

These lines are the key to a great deal in Mark 11–15. The special calling of the people of God, Mark implies, was to prepare the way for the coming of salvation in Jesus. At the time of the harvest they were to prove unfaithful by rejecting him and bringing about his death. The fig-tree which bore no fruit will be judged unworthy.

## The clearing of the temple market (11:15–19)

The incident of the fig-tree was apparently witnessed only by the apostles. The next action of Jesus had a wider audience.

> The service of the temple required markets where people could buy the animals and birds they needed to offer in sacrifice. Four such markets had existed for a long time on the Mount of Olives, but a fifth market had recently been opened by the high priest Caiphas in that part of the temple to which non-Jews were admitted. Moreover, the temple tax (which had to be paid at the latest by a fortnight before the Passover) could only be paid in a special currency, either the old Jewish currency or the Tyrian currency which most resembled it; and therefore money-changing desks were needed to change the usual Roman currency into temple coins. The result of all this was to make the Court of the Gentiles into a marketplace.

Jesus reacts with unusual violence and with great boldness. Within the precincts of the temple itself, where the chief priests are in charge, he takes for himself an authority which challenges theirs, and accuses them of betraying their guardianship of Israel's holy place. Mark justifies Jesus's action by a double quotation from Scripture: from Isaiah 56:7 –

And the foreigners who join themselves to the Lord ...
these will I bring to my holy mountain, and make
them joyful in my house of prayer ...

and from Jeremiah 7:11 –

Has this house, which is called by your name,
become a den of robbers?

Chapter 7 of Jeremiah continues: *Because you have done all these things, says the Lord, and when I spoke persistently you did not listen, and when I called on you you did not answer, therefore ... I will do to the house you called by my name ... as I did to Shiloh ... and I will cast you out of my sight.* The action of Jesus represents not only a religious concern for the holiness of a sacred place, but also a warning, a prophecy, a judgement, which is in fact felt by the chief priests and scribes as a threat. *They heard him* and *sought a way to destroy him.* The warning which these words implied was spoken in another way the next morning, when the fig-tree which bore no fruit was seen to be *withered away to its roots.* (11:20)

> Divide yourselves into Pharisees, Sadducees, Herodians, scribes as you did in chapter 3, and discuss the action of Jesus in the Temple from the point of view of the group you represent. (NB: the *chief priests* were Sadducees)

## The Parable of the Vineyard (12:1–12)

Far from taking back his words in the face of this challenge from the authorities, Jesus drives home the point he had been making the previous day, this time through a parable.

Like all parables, it belongs by its story to the time and the place.

> The vine was one of the two commercially most important cultivated plants in Palestine (the other was the olive). The features mentioned would be very familiar; the hedge was to protect the vineyard against animals and thieves, and the tower was a watchtower for security. The grapes were trodden down with the bare feet to tread out the juice; hence the *pit*. Judaea was especially a vine-growing province, and there are many traces in place-names and in archaeological remains of the vineyards which supplied grapes and wine for the city of Jerusalem and for the temple cult. It was common practice to let out a vineyard and to collect rent in kind.

But as so often it contains echoes from the Old Testament which need to be recaptured for the full meaning to emerge. The most important echo is of Isaiah 5:1–7:

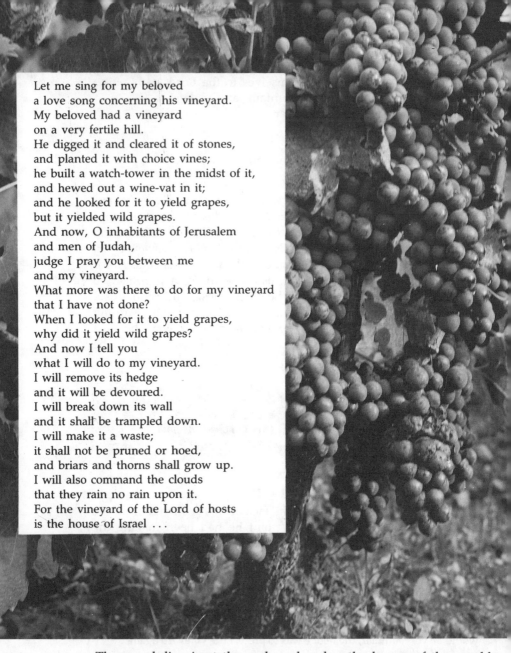

Let me sing for my beloved
a love song concerning his vineyard.
My beloved had a vineyard
on a very fertile hill.
He digged it and cleared it of stones,
and planted it with choice vines;
he built a watch-tower in the midst of it,
and hewed out a wine-vat in it;
and he looked for it to yield grapes,
but it yielded wild grapes.
And now, O inhabitants of Jerusalem
and men of Judah,
judge I pray you between me
and my vineyard.
What more was there to do for my vineyard
that I have not done?
When I looked for it to yield grapes,
why did it yield wild grapes?
And now I tell you
what I will do to my vineyard.
I will remove its hedge
and it will be devoured.
I will break down its wall
and it shall be trampled down.
I will make it a waste;
it shall not be pruned or hoed,
and briars and thorns shall grow up.
I will also command the clouds
that they rain no rain upon it.
For the vineyard of the Lord of hosts
is the house of Israel . . .

The punch-line is at the end, and makes the lesson of the parable clear. *He (the master) will come and destroy the tenants, and give the vineyard to others* (Mk 12:9). Leadership will pass from those who have been unfaithful to the very ones whom they reject, as builders might reject a stone which they consider worthless, but which in fact is perfectly shaped to support a corner (see Psalm 118:21,22). *They* (that is, presumably, the chief priests and scribes and elders of 11:27) are not slow to grasp the point of the parable *told against them*. They do not dare take up the challenge openly (*they left him and went away*). But the incident which follows shows them finding a less direct way of attacking Jesus.

In a number of different ways since his arrival in Jerusalem, Jesus has suggested that the spiritual leadership of God's people is to taken away from the religious authorities of his day. Make a list of all these occasions. In your role as Pharisees, Sadducees and so on, say how you react to this. Among which group or groups would you expect the strongest opposition to Jesus?

## A conflict of words (12:13–37)

They do so, says Mark, by asking Jesus some very awkward questions. The first question turns on a point of law. *Is it lawful to give tribute to Caesar or not?* The question was set *to entrap him* by two groups of people, Pharisees and Herodians, sent together for this purpose.

Look back to pp. 31, 32 and refresh your memory concerning the viewpoint of the Pharisees and the Herodians. Can you show why, whether he answers Yes or No, Jesus is bound to offend one of these groups?

The neat answer evades the trap, and they are *amazed*.

The second question was put to him by the Sadducees, very conservative people who accepted only the first five books of the Old Testament. Because in these books there is no expression of faith in a life after death, the Sadducees did not believe in a final resurrection. The question was designed to ridicule the very idea. Jesus sets aside the question itself, because it was not serious, but uses it to attack their fundamental disbelief. And he does this with a quotation from the book of Exodus – one of the five books which the Sadducees did accept.

The third question is different. The questioner seems to be sincere. There were supposed to be over 600 commandments within the Jewish law, and questions concerning their relative importance were often debated by the rabbis.

The first part of Jesus's reply is a quotation from the Book of Deuteronomy, chapter 6:

> Hear O Israel
> the Lord your God is one God;
> and you shall love the Lord your God
> with all your heart
> and with all your soul
> and with all your might.
> and these words which I command you
> shall be upon your heart,
> and you shall teach them diligently to your children,
> and you shall talk of them when you sit in your house,
> and when you walk by the way,
> and when you lie down and when you rise.

These were words which every Jew knew by heart, repeated in his morning and evening prayer, and wrote up on the doorpost of his house so that he might touch them as he came in and out. In other words, they were the very foundation of his religious life, expressing the relationship of love binding him always to God. And to them Jesus adds the commandment *You shall love your neighbour as yourself,* which is found in the Book of Leviticus 19:18.

Once again Jesus's reply goes beyond the question. Still basing his argument on the Books of the Law, he refuses to weigh commandment against commandment, but goes straight to the relationship of love which all the commandments took for granted, and which, if truly lived, made them all unnecessary.

And then Jesus asks a question in his turn. He quotes Psalm 110:1, which was generally thought to have been written by David and to refer to the Messiah. The question – which the opponents of Jesus either could not or would not answer – was how the Messiah could be at one and the same time David's son and David's Lord.

In itself, there was nothing unfriendly about shooting questions at a rabbi. It was an accepted way of drawing out his wisdom, and became even a form of popular entertainment (like *Mastermind* today). Four standard types of question were asked on these occasions: the 'wisdom' question, which turned upon a point of law; the 'scripture' question, concerning apparent contradictions in passages of Scripture; the 'mocking' question, which does not really seek an answer but aims at making fun of the rabbi's belief; and the 'moral' question, concerned with the principles of a moral or successful life.

(a) Can you show that the four questions in this section belong to these four categories?
(b) What phrase in Mark's account suggests a kind of popular entertainment?
(c) What phrase gives a much more sinister slant to the whole scene, and makes it part of the build-up of feeling against Jesus which Mark sees as preparing his arrest?

The denunciation of the scribes by Jesus (vv. 38–40) heightens the impression of conflict. These words of Jesus need not be in their historical position here – the phrase *and in his teaching he said* has no time-reference – but remembering them here Mark underlines the impression of opposition which he has already created.

*Note* On the whole the scribes were drawn from the poorer classes, and lived largely on the hospitality of pious people. When these were widows who were not well-off, they could not really afford to give hospitality to the scribes.

The mention of widows is a *catch-word* link with the next little incident. Against the wall of the court of the women in the temple were thirteen collection boxes, shaped like trumpets, into which people put their offerings for the temple treasury. This story stands by itself as a lesson on what truly makes a gift a generous one.

## Disaster ahead (Mk 13)

For a modern reader chapter 13 of Mark's gospel is difficult to understand. It falls into four sections:

A. *vv. 1–2* Jesus foretells the destruction of the temple. The temple of Jesus's time was a very striking building: its central part was covered with gold, and the rest of the building faced with yellow, blue and white marble. The Jewish historian Josephus says that *its fineness was incredible to those who had not seen it, and amazing to those who had*. For the pious Jew it was the holiest place on earth, and to say anything against it was like speaking against God. It was totally destroyed by the Romans in AD 70.

B. *vv. 3–23* In reply to the disciples' question *When?* Jesus answers: *The end is not yet*.

The description in this section of what believers would have to suffer must have sounded very familiar to Mark's first readers. The Christians of Mark's day knew what it was to be delivered up to councils (that is, local Jewish magistrates' courts); to be beaten in synagogues (where flogging was the punishment for disobedience or heresy); and to stand before governors and kings (the pagan authorities). Indeed, Jesus himself, as Mark will describe in chapter 15, suffered these very things. These verses would bring great comfort to the Christians of Rome, who would feel that their trials, like those of Jesus before them, were taken into God's plan and would bring them, like Jesus, through to glory.

One phrase needs explanation for the modern reader. Jesus gives one sign of the approach of particularly violent disaster. *When you see the desolating sacrifice set up where it ought not to be* .... What does this mean?

The expression is borrowed from the Old Testament Book of Daniel, of which there are many echoes in this chapter. In the year 168 BC the Syrian king Antiochus Epiphanes, having conquered Jerusalem, set up a heathen altar to Zeus in the Temple. To the Jews this was a terrible thing (they would not allow any image, let alone a pagan image, into the temple area) and Daniel calls it an *abomination* and a *desolation* (Dan. 12:11). What is Mark referring to?

We know of three similar attempts during the first century AD. In AD 26 (that is, during Jesus's own lifetime) when Pontius Pilate was made governor of Judaea, he ordered the Roman garrison to set up Roman banners, bearing the Roman eagle, within the temple boundaries. Because he feared a demonstration, he ordered it to be done by night. When the people saw them there the next morning, they organised a great protest march to Pilate's residence in Caesarea (nearly 100 miles) to beg him to remove the banners. Pilate marshalled the demonstrators into the great stadium, surrounded them with soldiers, and threatened to kill them all if they did not abandon the demonstration and go home. The Jews lay down on the ground and bared their throats to the soldiers' swords, declaring that they would rather die than see their temple desecrated. In the face of this non-violent passive resistance, Pilate gave in.

In AD 39 the Emperor Caligula gave orders that his statue should be set up in the temple in Jerusalem. The proconsul Petronius authorised a deputation of Jews to go to Rome and protest; but before a final decision could be arrived at, Caligula was murdered, and the idea was quietly dropped.

Some take the words in verse 14 as referring to this. But most take them as a reference to the desecration of the temple by Roman troops before its destruction in AD 70. This would make sense too of the reference to *flight*; when not only the temple but Jerusalem itself was sacked in AD 70, many Christians fled from the city and settled in Pella, across the Jordan.

## C. vv. 24–27: the coming of the Son of Man

These verses use symbolic imagery, very like that used in the Book of Daniel, to describe the End-time when God's justice will finally triumph in the coming of the Son of Man.

A key to a better understanding of these verses, and indeed of the whole chapter, has been given to scholars during the last hundred years. A number of books have come to light, all written between 200 BC and AD 200, which show that a certain kind of literary composition, known as an *apocalypse* (from a Greek word meaning *revelation*) was very much in fashion in Jewish and early Christian circles at that time. It was a kind of resistance literature, and was a product of the extreme violence and persecution suffered by the Jews at the hands of their (in turn) Syrian, Greek and Roman conquerors. Some thought that the only hope of freedom lay in armed resistance, and they banded together in guerrilla groups. But others still had a spiritual hope, that the God who had guided and protected them in the past would one day intervene, through the coming of a mysterious figure called the *Son of Man*, and set up a kingdom of justice which would be for ever.

An *apocalypse* was a book written to encourage this hope; and for this it had a special technique. The language was symbolic, possibly because, as resistance literature, it was safer if the outsider could not understand it. There were recognised and agreed symbols: an earth-shattering event, for example, was described in terms of cosmic disaster: suns turning black, stars falling from heaven and so on. (Notice that we have similar conventions of language ourselves:

when we say that an event is *earth-shattering* we do not necessarily mean that it literally caused an earthquake.) One such piece of writing, the Book of Daniel, was well-known to Mark's readers, and it is easy to recognise some of its expressions echoed in Mark 13. But there are other Old Testament echoes too.

Get hold of a copy of the Old Testament, look up the following passages, and copy out any expressions which you think are paralleled in Mark 13:24–7. (The Old Testament is not one book, but many. Use the Table of Contents to find the particular book you are looking for.)
(a) Book of Daniel 7:13–14
(b) Book of Isaiah 24:23
(c) Book of Joel 2:30–31
(d) Book of Ezekiel 32:7, 8.

Scholars have always recognised these echoes of the Old Testament in Mark 13. But the study of the recently-discovered apocalyptic writings has shown that such picture-language had become the stock-in-trade in this kind of literature. It led scholars to think that Mark may have had among his sources a short piece of writing of this kind, which he inserted into the gospel here; and because of its style, they began to refer to chapter 13 as the *little apocalypse*.

But when the excitement of this discovery began to pass, it became obvious that it is not quite so simple. Mark is not the kind of writer who copies unthinkingly from his sources, and if he has borrowed from a document of this kind, he does so only insofar as it serves his present purpose. Study of the language, of the words and style, show that it is not all borrowed. A great deal of this chapter is in Mark's own style, and many scholars think that much of it faithfully records the words of Jesus himself. What is most significant is that the overall purpose of this chapter is different from that of an apocalypse.

To see this clearly, we move on to:

D. *vv. 28–37: an exhortation to watchfulness*

The image of the fig-tree suggests that the signs of the times are to be read and understood. But the little parable of the master who returns unexpectedly emphasises that *you do not know when the time will come*. So the final lesson of the chapter, the final answer to the apostles' *When?* is: *Take heed . . . watch . . . Be prepared.*

In this respect Mark 13 is not an apocalypse. An apocalypse foretold what would surely take place, and all you had to do was to wait for it. But Mark tells his readers that they have more to do than that; they have to be patient, surely, and endure, but above all they have to watch. Notice how often this idea recurs. The whole chapter becomes a kind of farewell speech in which Jesus warns of troubles to come, promises final victory, but urges watchfulness and fidelity meanwhile.

(a) Make a list of all the places where the idea of watchfulness is mentioned in this chapter. Do you agree that this is Mark's main emphasis?

(b) Look up 13:30. Some people think, from this sentence, that Jesus, together with many Jews of his day and many early Christians, expected the Day of the Lord, the End-time, to happen very soon. What do you think of this idea?

# 8 Climax: the passion narrative
## (Mk 14 and 15)

Mark now proceeds rapidly with the story of the sufferings (often called the Passion) of Jesus, and his death. The events of the next few days were of the greatest importance to the Christian community. It was their belief that the full meaning of Jesus's life was revealed in his death, and that what at the time must have seemed to his followers the ultimate failure and the destruction of all their hopes was in reality the greatest act of love, and for Jesus the path to glory. Obviously the memory of this event was greatly prized by the early Christian community, and its story told again and again before Mark wrote it down.

Mark dates his narrative two days before the Passover feast, which according to his calendar was the Wednesday. The chief priests and scribes *were seeking how to arrest him by stealth* (14:1–2) and Judas Iscariot goes to them with an offer of betrayal. The facts are briefly told, with no attempt to analyse people's motives.

> Look back over the material discussed in the last chapter (Mk 11:1 – 13:37). Show how incident after incident has built up the picture and increased the tension, so that it does not come as a surprise that the chief priests and scribes resolve to take some action against Jesus.

Into this cold story of betrayal Mark inserts the incident of the anointing of Jesus with *nard*, a perfumed ointment which was one of the luxury goods traded in Jerusalem. Neither Mark nor Matthew names the woman who so anointed him; John later will identify her with Mary, sister of Martha, who lived in Bethany, and will locate the incident in her house. The significance of the story for Mark lies in the fact that the bodies of the dead were anointed; and Jesus, in defending her action, relates it to his approaching death. It is one of those little touches by which Mark shows Jesus as apparently in control as he goes towards his end.

## The Last Supper (14. 12–31)
The last meal which Jesus was to eat with his friends before he died, says Mark, was the Passover meal of unleavened bread, a lamb which had been sacrificed, and bitter herbs.

> Look up the description of the Feast of the Passover on p. 75. Discuss what significance Christians might see in the fact that Jesus's death took place on the celebration of the Passover.

Mark continues to emphasise Jesus's mastery over the events which were to master him. He is the *Teacher* who has only to ask to obtain the room he needs for himself and his friends. (The sight of a man carrying a pitcher of water, by the way, would have been unusual; normally the fetching and carrying of water would be a woman's task, as it still is in those parts of the world where a water-supply is not laid on.) At table he again foretells, in greater detail, that he will be betrayed by one of his friends.

Verses 22–5 were very important to the early Christian community, as they still are to every Christian community today. They show Jesus inserting actions and words into the ritual of the Passover meal so as to link his death with that which the Passover meal commemorated. We have seen (p. 75) how the Passover meal not only called to mind how the Jews were freed from the slavery of Egypt, but also made this liberation actual for all who shared the meal. It expressed their faith that a man's passage from slavery to real freedom is due to the working-out in his life (as in history) of the saving love of God to which he responds. Jesus's words *Take, this is my body* and *This is my blood of the covenant which is poured out for many* relate the sacrifice of his death and the pouring out of his blood to this saving action of God. From this moment on, for his followers, all that the *bringing out of Egypt* meant for the Jews is accomplished for all men and all times by the passing-over of Jesus, in an act of love, from this life to new life with his Father. After his death and resurrection, those who believe in him will make real for themselves this saving love, will realise his continued presence in faith among them, as they repeat his action in the *breaking of bread*. This is the origin and meaning of the central act of Christian worship under its various names of *Eucharist, Communion Service, Lord's Supper* or *Mass*.

**The arrest (14:32–52)**
The hymn referred to in verse 26 would be Psalm 118, which normally concluded the Passover ritual. Crossing the valley of Kedron to the Mount of Olives, Jesus again speaks of the approaching crisis, using the words of the prophet to foretell the behaviour of the apostles. At the same time he speaks of his resurrection, and refers to Galilee as the place where they will be reunited. Peter, impulsive as always, protests that he in any case will never desert Jesus; and Jesus foretells that in fact Peter will deny him *before the cock crows twice*.

The *place called Gethsemane* was one of the olive groves on the slope of the Mount of Olives which faces Jerusalem. There Jesus experiences great fear and depression at the prospect of what lies ahead. His friends are no support to him; his only support is in prayer. His prayer, as Christian tradition has preserved it, is very simple: a prayer to be spared, and a prayer of acceptance. The word *Abba* which begins his prayer is perhaps the most significant word in the New Testament. It is an Aramaic word, that is a word from the native language of Jesus's own country. Mark translates it into Greek: *Father*. It is unlikely that Mark or any other Jew would have dared to address God in this way unless Jesus himself had done so. Wherever therefore it is found in the gospels scholars presume that the evangelist is giving us the real words of Jesus himself.

According to Mark, the men who came to arrest Jesus were sent by *the chief priests and the scribes and the elders*, that is, by the Sanhedrin (see p. 92) who had the Temple guard at their disposal and were responsible for maintaining order in the city. Judas gives the pre-arranged signal of a kiss, apparently to make sure that in the darkness and confusion they do not arrest the wrong man. Jesus himself stops the attempt at armed resistance (according to John it was Peter who drew his sword, but none of the synoptic gospels identify him) and allows himself to be led away *that the scriptures might be fulfilled*. The curious incident of the young man who ran away naked is told only by Mark; this has led people to wonder whether he might not have been John Mark himself, who, as we know from Acts 12:12, had his home in Jerusalem.

**The trial of Jesus (14:53–15:15)**
Some knowledge of the political and legal situation in Palestine is needed as background to Mark's account.

Judaea at this time was governed directly by Rome in the person of the procurator, Pontius Pilate, whose residence was in Caesarea. During the days of pilgrimage, however, when the large numbers of people coming to Jerusalem could give rise to disturbances, Pilate would move into Jerusalem and live either in the old palace of Herod or with the garrison in the Fortress of Antonia, which overlooked the temple area from the north.

But although Pilate governed Palestine, and was responsible for keeping the peace there, it was not Roman policy to enforce the criminal and civil law directly. This task they left to a local Jewish institution, the Sanhedrin, or Supreme Court of Law. It was made up of 71 members, of whom 23 had to be present for its judgements to be legal. They were (a) chief priests, i.e. the high priest, previous high priests, and at least five others; (b) elders: that is, wealthy land-owners representing influential lay families in Jerusalem; (c) scribes, representing the Pharisee school of opinion. These were trained in the law of Moses, and could be considered legal experts.

The information we have concerning the Sanhedrin and its way of operating comes from a code (the *Mishna*) dating from AD 200, and we can only presume that what it says applied by and large in Jesus's day. There was no such arrangement as detention on remand, so trial generally followed close on the arrest.

The Sanhedrin met in the inner forecourt of the temple, and could not legally meet during the night, or on the eve of the sabbath or of a feast-day. There was no official prosecutor; the witnesses served as prosecution. The accused could be acquitted on the evidence of one witness, but for his condemnation two witnesses had to tell the same story. The Sanhedrin could judge capital offences under Jewish law, such as, for example, blasphemy. The punishment for blasphemy was stoning to death. There is some evidence that at the time of Jesus the Romans had taken from the Sanhedrin the power to carry out a capital sentence.

Political offences, and charges against Roman citizens, were dealt with not by the Sanhedrin, but by the Roman procurator, who at the time of Jesus was Pontius Pilate.

We know a good deal about Pilate. He was procurator of Judaea from AD 26 to 36. He seems to have had very little understanding of the kind of people he was asked to govern. We have already seen (pp. 85–6) that he blundered badly at the beginning of his period of office, and had to draw back in the face of determined passive resistance. Later on he made a similar mistake by putting up gilded tablets bearing the name of the emperor in the palace of Herod. The Jews protested and he took no notice. So they appealed over his head to the emperor, who told Pilate to remove the tablets. Once he took money from the temple treasury to build a water-conduit into Jerusalem. There was a demonstration. But he had planted soldiers out of uniform in the crowd, and on a signal they drew their swords and killed a large number of Jews. None of these events counted in his favour with the emperor, for the Empire needed a peaceful Palestine so that communications with the corn supplies of Egypt might be easy. Three years after the death of Jesus, Pilate was removed from office when the Sanhedrin formally complained to Caesar of his brutality.

The Roman procurator was sole judge in his court (not like the

Sanhedrin, where there was a bench of judges). He had the power to condemn a man to death and carry out the sentence. The normal mode of execution for non-Romans and for slaves was crucifixion; criminals were either tied or nailed to a cross and left to hang until they died of suffocation. This could be hastened by the breaking of their legs, which would throw the whole weight of the body on the arms and make breathing impossible. Another form of punishment was flogging. The instruments used were whips of leather thongs split lengthwise and fitted with pieces of bone or lead. There was no limit to the number of strokes given, and criminals, who were tied naked to a post, often collapsed and died from pain and loss of blood. Scourging was a punishment for various crimes, and was often given before executing a death sentence.

With this background information you are now in a position to answer for yourselves some key questions about the trial of Jesus:

(a) What judicial body is obviously referred to by the expressions *all the chief priests and the elders and the scribes* (14:53) and *the chief priests and the whole council* (14:55)?

(b) What specific charge was brought against Jesus? Why was it a serious charge?

(c) Why could Jesus not be convicted on the evidence of witnesses?

(d) How did the high priest break the deadlock?

(e) What crime was Jesus finally declared guilty of by the Sanhedrin?

(f) What details in Mark's narrative have led some to question the legality of the trial?

(g) What do you think might have been the purpose of the *consultation* of the next morning? (15:1)

(h) Why did the Sanhedrin take Jesus to Pilate?

(i) The charge aginst Jesus seems to have been changed when they did so. There is no longer a charge of blasphemy, but he is accused of having called himself King of the Jews. What do you think is the reason for this change?

(k) How did Pilate try to get out of sentencing Jesus?

(l) Who, in Mark's account, really wanted the death of Jesus, and were finally responsible for his condemnation?

(m) According to Pilate's record, he was not generally anxious to *satisfy the crowd.* Why do you think he might have decided to give in on this occasion?

## Execution (15:16–47)

The behaviour of the soldiers once Jesus had been condemned was probably typical. Excavation has uncovered a great stone-flagged area on the site of the Fortress of Antonia which may be connected with this scene. Scratched deep into the stone flags is a design which looks like a gaming-board, and a capital B (the Greek word for *king* is *Basileus*) suggests the 'Game of the King' with which the soldiers would have whiled away their time while on watch.

The crucifixion is told simply and factually, with no attempt to over-dramatise or play on the emotions. Details are authentic. The fact that Jesus had to be *helped* (v. 21) to carry the cross-bar to the place of execution imples that he was very weakened by the scourging he had received. The man who helped him to carry the cross is named, and referred to as *the father of Alexander and Rufus*, as though Alexander and Rufus were known to the Christian community for which Mark was writing. (Paul mentions a *Rufus* among the Christians of Rome to whom he was writing: see Romans 16:13.)

> Do you know anything about the work of the Simon community, or of the Cyrenians – two groups who do similar work, and who have chosen to be named after Simon of Cyrene? If you can find out about them, why do you think they wanted to be so named?

The place of execution had by law to be outside the walls of the city. The name *Golgotha* or *Skull-place* probably described the shape of the hill.

Mark gives the time of execution as *the third hour*, that is, nine o'clock in the morning. This fits in well with what is known about the administering of Roman justice: trials were generally held very early in the morning, and execution followed without delay. The giving of wine and myrrh to drink was normal practice; the drink was a kind of anaesthetic. The belongings of the criminal went to the soldiers who carried out the execution. It was usual for a criminal to carry round his neck or have tied above his head the crime for which he had been condemned. The inscription *King of the Jews* shows clearly that Jesus was officially condemned for challenging the authority of Caesar.

At the beginning of this book (p. 20) were listed the main sources from which the gospel-writers obtained their material. A great deal of study has been done in an attempt to disentangle the various strands of Mark's narrative in this account of the passion, so as to see him at work and become sensitive to the purpose which guided him.

Scholars are generally agreed that his main source is a very early tradition of Jesus's sufferings and death, preserved in the Christian community from its very foundation, forming part of its central belief and message, and historically very reliable. Into this Mark has woven other traditions, not essential to the main story, but contributing in various ways to the whole.

> You can test this out for yourselves.
>     Look for the part played in the story by the following characters, and discuss what would be lost if their story were omitted: Simon Peter; Judas; the woman with the ointment; Pontius Pilate; the young man with the linen sheet; the Roman centurion.

Mark also drew on the Old Testament for passages which threw light on the meaning of all these events.

> Look up in the Old Testament the following passages. Write them out in a left-hand column, and in a right-hand column opposite, note any echoes you find of them in Mark's account of the sufferings and death of Jesus:
>
> Psalm 22:1–18      Psalm 55:20–21
> Psalm 27:12        Psalm 71:10
> Psalm 31:13        Psalm 109:2,3
> Psalm 35:4         Isaiah 52:13, 14 and 53:1–12

Yet even as they suppose that Mark had different sources available to him, scholars are struck by the unity of style throughout and the way the narrative is knit smoothly together. As usual, Mark does not merely stick different sources together, but weaves them into a whole so as to convey, not only what actually happened (though he is very concerned with that here) but also his understanding of the meaning of those events.

> Below are two of the main statements about Jesus which it has been suggested Mark is making by the way he tells the story of the passion.
>    Take each one in turn, read Mark's narrative very carefully, and write out the case for this interpretation. (You are given a few clues in each instance.)
> (a) Jesus is at the same time the victim of man's wickedness, and yet strangely in control of events (*Clues*: What forces are gathered against him? What defence does he have? how does he conduct himself? Does he seem to know or accept what is going to happen? Examine all that he says. What is your general impression?
> (b) His death is part of God's plan. (*Clue*: your main clue here is the use Mark makes of Scripture passages – some of which you have already analysed.)

Another important idea running through Mark's narrative is that the death of Jesus marks the final betrayal by the Jewish leaders of their God-given trust, and the opening of God's kingdom to all men and women. In this context verses 38 and 39 are important. The *curtain of the temple* was the veil separating the inner room, the *Holy of Holies*, from the rest of the temple. No one except the high priest had the right to pass through it, and that only once a year. But now, says Mark through this image, the order represented by the temple is no longer valid, and the death of Jesus means that no one is shut out from God.

The *centurion* was the Roman officer in charge of the soldiers who carried out the crucifixion. Mark begins his gospel with the words:

*The beginning of the good news of Jesus Christ, the Son of God.* At the end, it was a Roman soldier, a pagan, who, when Jesus's own people had turned against him, and his followers had all run away, gave testimony to his greatness in words which echo the beginning: *Truly this man was the Son of God* ... and this was the first time in Mark's gospel that a human being had uttered these words. For the gentile converts of Rome that would have been specially significant.

In contrast too with the faint-heartedness of the apostles is the fidelity of the women followers of Jesus, whom Mark names as *looking from afar.* And the man who saw to his burial was a *member of the council,* that is, of the Sanhedrin which has been depicted as so hostile to Jesus.

There was a difficulty about the burial. Jesus died *at the ninth hour,* that is, at 3 o'clock on the Friday afternoon. The sabbath began on Friday at 6 p.m., and on the sabbath day burial was forbidden. This is why Joseph of Arimathea so hurriedly asked permission to take down the body of Jesus and bury it – an act which, as Mark says, took courage, since it cannot have been easy for a man in his position to identify himself in this way with a common criminal. Mark notes that Pilate first made sure that he was really dead (an important note, because some people later tried to explain away the resurrection by suggesting that he had not really died). The burial had to be done quickly, without the customary anointing; the body was merely laid in a *linen shroud,* a strip of linen at least twice as long as the person was tall, which was laid under the body and then folded back over the head to cover the body from head to toe. The *tomb* was not a dug grave, but a kind of cave hewn out of the rock and closed by a stone, rather like a mill-stone in shape, which rolled down into a groove.

---

*Who was to blame for the death of Jesus?*
There is no doubt that Mark places the blame for the death of Jesus firmly on the shoulders of *the Jews* – and not only the Jewish authorities, but also the mass of the people. The Jewish authorities arrest him, they declare him guilty of death, take him to the Roman authorities with a trumped-up charge, and put pressure on Pilate through a mob demonstration to have him crucified. All this is in keeping with their attitude throughout the gospel (see 3:6) and their final attack on him is prepared and made more credible by the verbal attack which precedes it. Even those Jews who were his close followers deserted, betrayed and denied him when it came to the crunch, and it was left for a Roman soldier, a pagan, to recognise his greatness at the moment of his death.

The tendency to blame the Jews for the death of Jesus is as strong in Matthew's gospel and in Luke's and strongest of all in the last gospel to be written, that of John.

Its results have been tragic. Blaming the Jews for the death of Jesus has been made the justification for fierce anti-Jewish prejudice, for a display of anti-semitism in Christian Europe, which throughout the

(cont'd)

centuries has led to much persecution of the Jews and many massacres.
It took the Nazi holocaust of the last war to shock the Christian
churches into realising and confessing to a prejudice of which they
have so long been guilty. For this many of them have publicly
confessed their shame and their repentance.

The work of scholars has raised the question of whether the Jews
were really as responsible as the gospel accounts suggest. Scholars say
that:
(a) the so-called trial before the Sanhedrin was very unlike a trial, and
    does not follow the usual procedures. It was illegal to meet at night;
    to condemn a man out of his own mouth; and there was no reason
    why Jesus, so condemned, could not have been stoned as Jewish
    law prescribed.
(b) the picture of Pilate that emerges, that of a kindly but hesitant man
    yielding to public pressure, is totally unlike that which emerges
    from the pages of history.
A recent Jewish historian (Paul Winter: *On the Trial of Jesus*, 1974) has
argued that the gospel writers deliberately played down the part of the
Romans in the events connected with Jesus's death, and in so doing
laid an unfair proportion of blame on the Jews.
Why should they do so? Some possible explanations are:
(a) They had a religious-political motive. Mark was writing towards the
end of a four-year war between the Jews and the Empire, the climax of
years of uprisings and guerrilla warfare. The Romans had finally won;
but the Jews had fought with tenacity and suicidal courage, led by men
who were heroic in their resistance unto death. These men were the
villains of the piece in Roman eyes. Now the one indisputable fact
about Jesus's death was that he had been crucified, that is, put to death
by the Roman authorities. So he could easily be regarded, in far-away
Rome, as another of the terrorist anti-Roman leaders. Not only could

(cont'd)

this be very dangerous for his followers, but it could lead to a total misunderstanding of who he was and what he stood for. They therefore needed to show that although he was executed by the Romans, the real issue at stake was not a political one, but a religious one. He was the last and the greatest of the prophets who had been rejected by the very people they came to preach to. Telling the story of the passion from this angle meant emphasising the conflict between Jesus and his own people, and showing them therefore as responsible for his death.

The difficulty about this explanation is that it presumes that the gospel writers were the inventors of this anti-Jewish prejudice. In reality it had been expressed before the gospels were written. Paul, writing to the Christians of Thessalonika within twenty years of Jesus's death, wrote very harshly of the *Jews, who killed both the Lord Jesus and the prophets*. And it does not appear that he had any political motive.

(b)  Another explanation may lie, strangely enough, in the very fact that the first preachers of the Christian religion were themselves Jews by birth and by upbringing (Paul had been educated as a Pharisee). They did not immediately break with the main practices of their Jewish religion; only gradually did they realise that in following Jesus they would appear to other Jews as heretics preaching strange and unacceptable doctrines. For this they were beaten and thrown out of the synagogues. They suffered deeply from this. They felt cut off from so much in their past which had been good and holy.

Also, they felt let down. They had shared the belief that the Jewish people had been specially chosen by God, loved and educated and led by him throughout their history so that through them his salvation might come to all men. And so, when it became apparent that the Jews they lived among were not going to accept Jesus as the Christ, they really felt that the Jewish people had betrayed their destiny. And this hurt all the more because the Jews were their own people. It is when we have been let down by someone near to us that we most fiercely react. And they reacted in reproach and sometimes in bitter accusation.

(c)  Another reason may be found in the kind of preaching common in the early Church, as far as we can judge it from the sermons recorded in the Acts of the Apostles. We are told that wherever Paul went on his missionary journeyings through Asia Minor he tried first to convert to Christ the little colonies of Jews that had settled nearly everywhere in the civilised world. Now preachers often call people to repent by reminding them of their past sins; and these early preachers were no exception. So Peter, preaching in one of the porches of the temple, spoke of *Jesus, whom you delivered up and denied in the presence of Pilate, when he had decided to release him. But you denied the Holy and Righteous One . . . and killed the author of life . . . Repent then, and turn again . . .* (Acts 3:13–19). The Acts of the Apostles was written later than Mark's gospel, but the kind of preaching it describes was probably typical of preaching in the early Church.

What all this adds up to is:
(i)  that there is undoubtedly an anti-Jewish bias, growing stronger

(cont'd)

from gospel to gospel, in the accounts of the passion and death of Jesus;

(ii) that the gospel writers did not invent it, but consciously or unconsciously reinforced it;

(iii) that it arose out of a variety of experiences: fear, disillusionment (as Jews), missionary zeal . . .

Throughout the centuries this prejudice did not diminish, but has been partly responsible for a great deal of injustice and oppression.

Christians of today, seeing all this in the perspective of history, can both understand its origins and perceive its injustice. Realising that it is totally out of tune with the spirit of the Jesus they try to follow, they are struggling to free themselves from so deeply-ingrained a prejudice as they confess their guilt.

### What is prejudice?

Are you aware of being prejudiced against any group or groups of people? If so, what has given rise to this feeling in you? Do you think it can lead you to judge others unjustly?

Do you feel that any group to which you belong (e.g. youth . . . or a racial group . . .) is looked at by others with prejudice? Can you understand it? What would you like to say to the people who are prejudiced against you?

# 9 What is the good news according to Mark?

In all the gospels the climax of Jesus's passion and death is the resurrection. In the first eight verses of chapter 16 Mark shows how the women who loved and were faithful to Jesus received the first hint that the story is not finished. Early on the Sunday morning they go to the grave to anoint the body, since this had not been done on the Friday night. They find the large, heavy stone rolled to one side. A young man, *dressed in a white robe* (the colour of glory – compare the Transfiguration in 9:2–3) gives them two important messages for *the disciples and Peter*: that Jesus is risen, and that he will be reunited to them in Galilee *as he told you* (a reference to 14:28). The women, however, do not do as they are told; this news is so unexpected, so beyond their experience, that their reaction is *trembling and astonishment*, and they say nothing to anyone *for they were afraid*.

## The ending of Mark's gospel
The remaining verses of chapter 16 (16:9–20) are probably not part of Mark's gospel as he originally wrote it. Scholars have been led to this conclusion because:

> these verses are not included in some of the earliest manuscripts; their style is very different from that of the rest of the gospel – they are not written in the kind of Greek Mark usually writes; and what they contain is merely a summary of resurrection stories found in the other gospels.

On the other hand, the story of the women makes a strangely incomplete ending to the gospel. What happened next? If the women said nothing, how did the other followers of Jesus become convinced that he was risen? Moreover, though the English translation cannot show this, the last sentence in Greek ends with a conjunction, a joining-up word, which makes the sentence even as a sentence seem unfinished. For these reasons it seems probable that Mark did not finish his gospel here.

What then was the original ending? We do not know. It may well have been lost by the tearing away of the end of the scroll on which the gospel was originally written. Then later readers, seeing that it was incomplete, would have rounded it off by adding a brief summary taken from other writers. Though we do not know for sure, this book will presume that it was so, and postpone the study of 16:9–20 until the fuller version of those resurrection stories in the other synoptic gospels can be looked at.

## The message of Mark

To lose the end of a story could deprive the whole story of meaning, particularly if the ending contained an unexpected twist, a change in the fortunes of the hero, or the solution of a problem. Though it would have been interesting to know how Mark actually did bring his gospel to a conclusion, it is remarkable that the gospel is not deprived of meaning by the lack of an ending.

This is because for Mark the Good News is not just that the story of Jesus had a happy ending after all. That he is risen is an essential part of the good news; that he will come again is also part of it. But Mark has not waited until the end to affirm this good news. It is present on every page.

For throughout the gospel Mark has seen and described the earthly life of Jesus through the eyes of a believer. Without in any way

reducing the human reality of Jesus, who loved and was angry, who hungered, suffered disappointment, was afraid and reduced almost to despair, Mark sees him always as the one in whose person the victory over evil is present from the beginning.

He presents Jesus as a man with authority, an authority which puts evil to flight wherever and in whatever form he meets it. He teaches with authority, a profoundly wise teaching which cuts through petty arguments about law and reaches out to the deeper values of love and relationship with God and neighbour. He goes beyond the normal limits of sympathy; his love is open to strangers, to the despised, the sinner, the outcast; to women and to children.

He can be led beyond the narrow outlook of his own people, and proclaim, not only in words but also in action, that salvation is for all people.

Those who are closest to him constantly catch glimpses of this extra dimension of his personality, and once at least they see it so clearly that it is as though they are seeing in advance the light of his resurrection or of his coming in glory.

He can undergo suffering and death knowing that the inevitability of it is part of the saving plan of God. Therefore even as he is mastered by people and events he seems to remain master; he accepts betrayal, refuses armed protection, keeps dignity before his accusers, and finally dies a death which has universal meaning and marks the passing of the old order and the coming of a new, in which all those who believe can come to God through him.

His followers will be identified with him: they will tread the same path of suffering and self-denial, and carry within themselves the same glory and the same hope. One of them (Paul) had already written this truth as he had experienced it in his own life: *We are in difficulties on all sides, but never cornered; we see no answer to our problems, but never despair; we have been persecuted but never deserted; knocked down but never killed; always, wherever we may be, we carry with us in our body the death of Jesus, so that the life of Jesus too may be always seen in our body. Indeed, while we are still alive we are consigned to our death every day, for the sake of Jesus, so that in our mortal flesh the life of Jesus, too, may be openly shown.* (2 Cor. 4:8–11, *Jerusalem Bible trans.*)

The genius of Mark was to show a way of conveying this great conviction of Christianity, not by preaching a sermon, but by a certain way of writing the life of Jesus. He wrote, as we have seen, for a particular believing community at a particular time. Because for the most part they were converts from paganism, he emphasises that Jesus came to save, not only the Jews, but everyone. Because they were living in a hostile world, were rejected and persecuted, he knew that they could identify particularly with the sufferings and death of Jesus. But the essence of his message was for everyone and for all time. Throughout the gospel, as already in the first fourteen verses, he shows Jesus as the one who brings joy to men by fulfilling all the expectations of the Old Testament. He is in communion with God, whom he calls his father. God is with him; he enters the wilderness of life, meets the evil which is mingled with all human experience, conquers it and brings salvation. For his followers as for himself there is one way to that salvation: *Whoever would save his life will lose it, and whoever loses his life for my sake and for the gospel will save it.*

This is the message of Mark.

On p. 101 and on this page, a number of statements are made about Jesus as Mark presents him (from *Without in any way* . . . to . . . *the same glory and the same hope*). Each of these statements is based on at least one incident or one passage in the gospel of Mark. If you can give the appropriate reference in every case, you will know that your study of Mark's gospel has been very thorough, and that you have become really familiar with its text.

# MATTHEW

## 10 The gospel according to Matthew

To read the gospel of Matthew after reading that of Mark is to recognise immediately great similarities and great differences. Many passages are so alike that, if we accept Mark's as earlier, it is obvious that Mark's gospel was known to Matthew, and was one of his main sources. Other sections are completely new.

**The synoptic problem**

The attempt to discover how the three synoptic gospels relate to each other, and what written sources they used, is generally called the *synoptic problem*.

It is generally also accepted that both Matthew and Luke drew from an earlier collection of the *Sayings of Jesus*, generally referred to as Q from the German word for source (*Quelle*).

It is obvious too that Matthew has some material (especially in his first chapters) drawn from an unknown source which he alone uses; and that Luke also has some material from a different source again.

Whenever the four gospels are listed in early Church writings, the gospel of Matthew is named first. We know that it was the most widely-used and best known in the first centuries throughout the Church. These facts, together with the fact that it is the most 'Hebrew' of them all, led many to think that it was the first to be written. But the general opinion today places Mark's gospel first. The following are the main arguments for this:

(i)   Matthew reproduces nearly all Mark's subject-matter, and Luke reproduces over half of it. This is more easily explained by a dependence of Matthew and Luke upon Mark than vice versa.

(ii)  The order of events in Mark is followed generally by Matthew and Luke. Where Matthew departs from it, Luke follows it; and when Luke departs from it, Matthew follows it. Nowhere do Matthew and Luke agree against Mark, as one would expect them to do sometimes if Matthew were the first source.

(iii) Matthew has his own typical style and vocabulary, yet he uses 51 per cent of Mark's actual words. Luke writes polished Greek (very

(cont'd)

different from Mark's rougher style) yet he uses 50 per cent of
Mark's actual words.
(iv) Mark's style is the most vivid and he gives the most detail,
suggesting that he is nearest to the actual event.
(v) When Matthew's or Luke's account differ from what Mark had
written, it is often possible to see why. The changes are dictated by
the particular purpose of Matthew or of Luke. (We shall have
examples of this in the chapters which follow.)

Assuming that Mark's gospel was the earliest, the relationship of the
gospels to their written sources can be displayed in diagrammatic form:

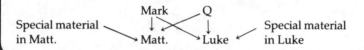

Where Matthew uses Mark, he does not merely copy. Just as Mark
felt free to choose from the stories and the teachings which were
available to him in the Church, and to use them so as to convey his
central message, so Matthew uses his sources with the same freedom.
Sometimes Matthew inserts into Mark's account material from
another source; sometimes he omits details which are not important
for his purpose; and sometimes he makes slight verbal changes which
do not affect the content of a story, but give it a different emphasis.
All these alterations, however slight, can be clues to the mind of
Matthew. So in this chapter we shall take some of the passages
Matthew has borrowed from Mark, see what he has done with them,
and relate the changes he has made to the main ideas which run
through his gospel.

## The New Israel

Compare closely Mk 1:2–8 and Matt. 3:1–12. Write out those verses in
Matthew which have no parallel in Mark.
    They include two mini-parables. Do you notice any similarity in the
meanings of these two parables?

You will have discovered that Matthew uses two images (that of an
unproductive fruit-tree cut down by the gardener, and that of the
useless chaff separated from wheat grains and thrown away) which
he addresses to the Pharisees and the Sadducees, that is, to the
religious leaders of the Jewish people. Towards the end of Mark's
gospel (see pp. 80 and 82) the Jewish leaders are condemned for being
unfaithful to their trust, and are warned that the spiritual leadership
of God's people would be taken from them. Through the preaching of
John the Baptist Matthew makes this same point from the very

beginning of his gospel. Some knowledge of the community for which Matthew was writing helps the reader to see why.

Matthew's gospel is thought to have been written, not for a Roman church with a majority of converts from paganism, but for a church much nearer to Jerusalem, where a large number of the Christians had been Jews by religion, as they were still Jews by race. And what was happening in Jewish circles was important. By this time (somewhere around AD 80) faithful Jews were recovering from the shock of the destruction of their holy city and their temple by the Romans in AD 70. They had to find new ways of worshipping God which were not centred on the temple, and which could be practised too by the colonies of Jews who were by that time scattered throughout the civilised world. Led by holy men like the Rabbi Johannan ben Zakkai and his successor Gamaliel (both Pharisees), they put their laws and traditions (even those which up to now had never been written down) into writing. They wanted particularly to keep the scattered members of their faith united in prayer and practice in spite of the fact that they were scattered far and wide.

In this anxiety they did not feel safe enough to tolerate groups that did not follow the main line – what we would call fringe groups. Little

Above it says that the Jews *did not feel safe enough to tolerate groups that did not follow the main line* . . .

From your observation of society today, do you think that when a group of people live and behave differently from the way most people live and behave, then, even if they do no one any harm, others feel afraid of them? Can you quote an example? Do you think there is a link between fear and intolerance?

by little it had become clear that the followers of Jesus (who had at first been thought of as merely an eccentric Jewish sect) held beliefs and practices which could not be reconciled with Jewish beliefs and practices; and they were also increasingly admitting gentiles into their fellowship. The reformed Jewish 'church' felt the need to state very clearly that these 'Christians' did not belong to them. They did so by inserting into the sabbath prayer-service a prayer which no Christian could say.

Many Jewish Christians were hurt by this. They had not wanted to break with the religion of their childhood, and would have been happier to continue to pray in the synagogues. But they were now shut out. So the gulf between Christians and Jews grew wider and feelings of opposition grew stronger. Matthew's gospel is particularly marked by this. He is deeply concerned to understand what the relationship can be in God's plan between the Jews, who represent the *Israel* of the Old Testament, and the *new Israel* formed of those who believe in Christ.

## What kind of kingdom?

One of the terms Matthew uses often to describe the new order established by Jesus is the phrase *the kingdom of heaven*, which occurs no less than thirty-two times in his gospel. Now compare Mark 1:12–13 with Matthew 4:1–11.

The brief picture Mark gives of Jesus encountering evil is expanded by Matthew into the dramatic story of how Jesus, at the beginning of his public life, has to make a fundamental choice concerning the kind of kingdom he is to establish. He is not called to serve his own well-being (vv. 3, 4) nor to dominate others and arouse popular enthusiasm by spectacular demonstrations of personal power (vv. 5–7); nor to aim at political power and sovereignty (vv. 8–10). The nature of his kingdom will emerge as Matthew's gospel proceeds.

## Fulfilment of prophecy

Another kind of insertion common in Matthew's gospel is illustrated by a comparison between Mk 1:14 and Matt. 4:15–16. Mark said simply that Jesus began his preaching in Galilee. Matthew expands this, introducing a quotation from the prophet Isaiah (Is. 9:1–2) and seeing the presence of Jesus in *Galilee of the Gentiles* as a fulfilment of that prophecy. This reference back to the Old Testament is something that Matthew does very often. Puzzling about the relationship between the New Israel and the Old, he is led to see it in terms of fulfilment. And he meditates on the Old Testament in this light until it seems to him that the Old Testament almost writes the gospel in advance.

## Teaching through miracle stories

So far we have looked at *additions* made by Matthew to the text of

Mark. *Omissions* and small verbal *alterations* can be no less significant. This becomes apparent if some of the miracle stories in Mark and Matthew are compared.

One way of doing this is to place them in parallel columns, as follows:

**Mark 2:1–12**

And when he returned to Capernaum after some days, it was reported that he was at home. And many were gathered together, so that there was no longer room for them, not even about the door, and he was preaching the word to them. And they came, bringing to him a paralytic carried by four men. And when they could not get near him because of the crowd, they removed the roof above him, and when they had made an opening, they let down the pallet on which the paralytic lay. And when Jesus saw their faith, he said to the paralytic, 'My son, your sins are forgiven'. Now some of the scribes were sitting there, questioning in their hearts, 'Why does this man speak thus? It is blasphemy. Who can forgive sins but God alone?' And immediately Jesus, perceiving in his spirit that they thus questioned within themselves, said to them, 'Why do you question thus in your hearts? Which is easier to say to the paralytic, Your sins are forgiven, or to say Rise, take up your pallet and walk? But that you may know that the Son of Man has authority on earth to forgive sins,' he said to the paralytic, 'I say to you, rise, take up your pallet and go home.' And he rose, and immediately took up the pallet, and went out before them all, so that they were all amazed, and glorified God, saying: 'We never saw anything like this.'

**Matt. 9:1–8**

And getting into a boat, he crossed over and came to his own city.

And behold, they brought to him a paralytic, lying on his bed.

and when Jesus saw their faith, he said to the paralytic, 'Take heart, my son, your sins are forgiven.' And behold, some of the scribes said to themselves, 'This man is blaspheming.'

But Jesus, knowing their thoughts

said: 'Why do you think evil in your hearts? Which is easier to say, Your sins are forgiven, or to say Rise and walk? But that you may know that the Son of Man has authority on earth to forgive sins,' he then said to the paralytic

'Rise, take up your bed and go home.'

And he rose,

and went home. When the crowds saw it, they were afraid and they glorified God who had given such authority to men.

Compare these two columns. It is obvious that Matthew's version is shortened. What kind of detail has he omitted? What has he kept almost word for word?

Now take Mk 5:25–34 and Matt. 9:20–22. Write them out for yourselves in parallel columns. Ask yourselves the same questions. In the light of your answers, see whether you agree with the conclusions of the next paragraph. If you disagree, say why.

**Conclusions** In these as in other miracle stories, Matthew omits many vivid details – the kind of details that make it sound like an eye-witness account. The result is to streamline the miracle story, to shift the attention from the healing and the person healed, and to focus on the person of Jesus and his teaching – teaching on forgiveness of sins in the first case, on faith in the second. In Mark's gospel Jesus appears above all as a worker of *mighty works* (so much so that Mark had to warn against thinking of him as some kind of magician). In Matthew he is above all a teacher, whose words have even greater authority than his deeds.

## Discipleship, faith and leadership

Sometimes the alterations Matthew makes are very small – so small as to seem unimportant. But even small verbal changes can make a difference to the feel of the story and its meaning. Compare for example:

| **Mk 4:35–41** | **Matt. 8:23–27** |
|---|---|
| On that day, when evening had come, he said to them: Let us go across to the other side. And leaving the crowd, they took him with them in the boat just as he was. | And when he got into the boat, his disciples followed him. |
| And a great storm of wind arose, and the waves beat into the boat, so that the boat was already filling. | And behold, there arose a great storm on the sea, so that the boat was being swamped by the waves, |
| But he was in the stern, asleep on the cushion; | but he was asleep. |
| and they woke him, and said to him, Teacher, do you not care if we perish? | And they went and woke him, saying: Save, Lord, we are perishing. |
| And he awoke and rebuked the wind, and said to the sea: Peace! Be still! and the wind ceased, and there was a great calm. He said to them: Why are you afraid? Have you no faith? | And he said to them: Why are you afraid, men of little faith? Then he arose and rebuked the winds and the sea, and there was a great calm. |
| And they were filled with awe, and said to one another: Who is this, that even wind and sea obey him? | And the men marvelled, saying: What sort of man is this, that even winds and sea obey him? |

Matthew's alterations seem very slight. As usual, his version is shorter, and 'eye-witness' details like the cushion are omitted. At first sight, however, his alterations seem insignificant. Mark says that the disciples *took him (Jesus) with them in the boat*; Matthew that they *followed* Jesus. Matthew has altered the words with which they wake Jesus, and the order of the dialogue which follows. Do these changes make any real difference?

The clue is in the context. What precedes this miracle in Matthew is a dialogue between Jesus and some individuals who were thinking of becoming his disciples. A scribe said: *Teacher, I will follow you wherever you go* ... Jesus said: *Follow me, and leave the dead to bury their own dead. And when he got into a boat, his disciples followed him.* In Mark the emphasis of the story was on Jesus's authority. Matthew makes it a story about the response to that authority, which is a *following* – it becomes a story, that is, about discipleship. This is why, whereas in Mark the disciples reproach Jesus for sleeping, in Matthew, like true followers, they *pray* to him. (*Lord, save* was an official form of Christian prayer.) Faith is essential to a follower: and so in Matthew Jesus stops to reproach them for their *little faith* before stilling the storm. Matthew's interest is obviously not so much in the miracle itself as in the behaviour of the disciple in crisis.

Once one begins this process of comparison, all kinds of interesting things come up. Take Mk 6:47–52 and Matt. 14:22–33. The stories are identical in their opening sentences; their endings are quite different.

In Mark (and this fits the context, you may remember) the disciples *were utterly astounded, for they did not understand ... their hearts were hardened*. In Matthew, where the disciples are models of what a disciple should be, *they worshipped him, saying: Truly, you are the Son of God.*

It may be surprising to find that this is one miracle told at much greater length by Matthew than by Mark. Copy out those verses which are only in Matthew, and you can see that Matthew has inserted the episode about Peter walking on the waters. He even uses a different word for the sea of Galilee in these verses: he calls it *the water* instead of *the sea* (two different Greek words are used). This suggests that it comes from another source: Mark's word is always the one here translated *the sea*. But this memory of Peter walking on the waters was important to Matthew. It is thought that the Christian community for which he was writing was the Church at Antioch in Syria, where Peter had been a very important figure.

Hunt up all the references to Peter, first in Mark's gospel and then in Matthew's (You can share out the research.)

From the result of your research compare the two pictures of Peter which emerge.

Discuss your findings in reference to the fact that Peter had been a leading figure in the church at Antioch, and then went to Rome, where his memories may have been one of Mark's sources.

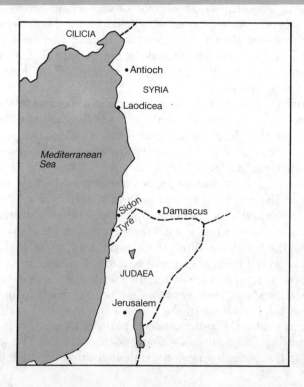

*Note* The supposition that Matthew wrote his gospel for the Christian church at Antioch in Syria has very strong backing. Study of the gospel itself shows that it was written for a Greek-speaking community, a well-developed and well-organised Church, with a strong Jewish element in tension with a leadership which had fully accepted a gentile Christianity. Antioch fits this bill.

We know that Antioch had a large Jewish colony as early as the second century BC. A Christian mission was founded there as early as AD 40 (see Acts 11:19–20). The church leaders in Jerusalem sent Barnabas there to oversee the new development; and it was there that the followers of Jesus were first called *Christians*. There gentiles were from the beginning received into the church without first becoming Jews; and when a great meeting was held in Jerusalem to discuss whether this should be so, Barnabas and Paul went there from Antioch to explain why they had been doing this.

The meeting decided that gentiles should indeed be admitted without circumcision, but that all should be asked to observe certain Jewish food laws, so that those who had been brought up as Jews would not be disgusted.

A passage in Paul's letter to the Galatians (ch. 2) shows that this decision did not solve all difficulties. Two parties still remained, one very liberal and open, the other still attached to Jewish traditional practices. Paul is very critical of Peter. He says that Peter had no difficulty at first about eating with gentile converts, but later stopped doing so when people from the influential traditional party arrived from Rome and criticised him.

The church at Antioch seems to have got over this difficult moment and continued to prosper. Antioch escaped the full force of the Roman invasion of AD 70, and the Christian church there survived. As a large urban centre with a well-organised church, it would have been able to give Matthew's gospel the backing which made it what it became by the second century – the best-known and most widely used gospel of all. The early Christian writer Ignatius of Antioch certainly knew and used Matthew's gospel about AD 100.

## The Canaanite woman (Matt. 15:1–39)

Look back now over pp. 00 and refresh your memory concerning the significance of Mark 7:1 – 8:10. The message of this passage, relevant in Rome, would be even more relevant to the divided community at Antioch. You will not be surprised therefore to find that Matthew, chapter 15 reproduces it almost word for word.

But not quite; Matthew has made a few changes. Make a list of them. Can you show that their effect is to make the point even sharper? (One clue: to see why Matthew has substituted verses 31 and 32 for the miracle of the deaf and dumb man, look up Isaiah 61:1–2 and Luke 7:18–33.)

What is the force of these alterations? In Matt. 3:9 John the Baptist had rebuked those who prided themselves on being descended from

Abraham, and had said that *God could from these stones raise up children to Abraham*. Paul had already written to the Christians of Galatia (a town in Asia Minor) that *the true children of Abraham are the children of his faith*. Matthew in this miracle story declares, even more strongly than Mark, that this is true, and that this pagan woman has, by her faith, become one of the lost sheep of the House of Israel, and entitled to the mercy of her Lord.

Look up Matt. 8:5–13 for another miracle story, not told by Mark, which conveys the same message.

Examining some of the passages where Matthew is obviously using Mark as his source has drawn out some of Matthew's main themes: the Christian Church as the New Israel; the fulfilment of prophecy; the nature of the kingdom of God; discipleship. The chapters which follow will examine how Matthew also develops these themes by using other sources.

# 11 The values of the kingdom

So important to Matthew is the idea of the Christian Church as the *New Israel* that it may even have determined the shape of his gospel.

A great deal of Matthew's gospel is composed of what Jesus said, rather than what he did. Much of this material probably came from an earlier written collection of the *Sayings of Jesus* which were already well-known among Christians. It was customary for a rabbi's disciples to take notes of his oral teaching and circulate them as the 'Sayings of Rabbi So-and-so.' It would be normal for the followers of Jesus to do likewise. In any case, we have a good deal of evidence that such a collection existed.

## Jesus the new Moses

Five times in Matthew's gospel the author concludes a section with the phrase *And when Jesus had finished these sayings* . . . (see Matt. 7:28; 11:1; 13:53; 19:1; and 26:1). The five sections which end this way are:

Matt. 5–7:   The Sermon on the Mount
Matt. 10:   How the kingdom is to be preached
Matt. 13:   Parables of the kingdom
Matt. 18:   The community of believers, sign of the kingdom
Matt. 24–5:   More parables of the kingdom.

If the story-parts of the gospel are grouped around these teaching passages, the whole gospel can be seen to fall into five parts.

It is possible that this division had significance for Matthew. Men of the Old Israel had built their lives upon the Law, that is, the first five books of the Bible, which they believed expressed God's love for them and how they were to live in return for this love. They thought that these first five books had been given to them by Moses, who had passed on to them from God the ten commandments which he had received on the top of Mount Sinai. For Matthew, Jesus is like a new Moses founding the new Israel. Like those of Moses, the teachings of Jesus are here contained in five books. And his foundation commandments are given from a mountain, as were those of Moses.

## The Sermon on the Mount

In chapters 5–7 particularly, Matthew presents Jesus as the new Moses, a great teacher giving from the *mountain* the new law which is to govern men's lives. But it is not really a sermon, and it is most unlikely, to say the least, that Jesus said all these things on one occasion. But Matthew has gathered together a number of his sayings, and presented them here in one great 'manifesto'. The expression *he opened his mouth and taught them* introduces solemn and official teaching.

### The eight beatitudes

The first twelve verses are about happiness (*beatitude* comes from a Latin word meaning *happy*). They are short sayings with deep meaning, and they seem to turn upside down the values generally accepted in society. For Jesus they express the values on which his kingdom is to be founded, and by which his followers are invited to live. Jesus says that happiness is not to be found in riches and self-sufficiency, in pleasure-seeking, in power and violence, in living for oneself ... A few explanations can help with expressions unfamiliar to today's reader:

(a) The *poor in spirit* are those who know that they are *poor*, that is, that they do not have in themselves all that is needed for the fullness of their lives, but are open to receive from others, and especially from God. (It was an expression which had come to have meaning for those Jews particularly, who relied for their salvation not on armed rebellion against the Roman armies, but upon the faithfulness of God to his promises.)

(b) The *meek* are the gentle at heart, the non-violent.

(c) *Righteousness* is the right order of things, the way things ought to be within a man and around him. Jesus is saying that things like justice and peace are as important to people as are food and drink.

(d) The *pure in heart* are, for Jesus, those who go through life with their eyes fixed on God, who are single-minded in their pursuit of what is good.

(e) The *peace-makers* are not those who want peace at any price, but those who *make* peace, who build peace in a world of conflict.

(f) By the time this gospel came to be written, Jesus himself had known what it meant to be *persecuted for justice's sake*, and many of his followers had experienced it too.

At the end of the eight beatitudes Matthew places the little parable of the salt of the earth and the lamp on the lampstand, to illustrate the contribution made to mankind by those who have the courage to live according to his teaching.

1 Which of the beatitudes do you think are particularly important to our world today? Why?

2 Do you know of anyone, either from the past or alive today, whose life illustrates particularly any one of these beatitudes? Say why you think so.

### The new law (5:17–48)

Jesus appears in all the gospels as a good Jew. He seems to have observed the main practices of his religion, though he was very free with regard to petty observances: and even when he protested against too narrow and inhuman an interpretation of laws like that of the sabbath, he did not condemn the law itself.

Matthew must have had in mind, as he wrote, the Jewish Christians of Antioch, that is, Christians converted from the Jewish faith. The religion in which they had been brought up was a true and a good religion, and Matthew did not wish in any way to lead his readers to deny that goodness and truth. So before going any further with the moral teaching of Jesus, he includes a saying which makes clear Jesus's general position with regard to the Jewish law. The new Israel was to be a fulfilment of the old, and Jesus's teaching was to be the fulfilment of that which had guided the Jews through the centuries. *Think not that I have come to abolish the law and the prophets; I have not come to abolish them but to fulfil them.* This saying is central to Matthew's understanding of the relationship between Jesus's teaching and the Jewish faith.

This being said, it would seem that Jesus proceeds to set himself up as an authority over against the Jewish law. Six times he uses the formula: *You have heard that it was said of old ... but I say to you.* When the rabbis were teaching from the Torah (Law of Moses) and balancing one passage against another, they would use the formula: *It was said to men of old ... but learn also that it was said ...* So they quoted one passage against another, but would never have dared teach on their own authority. Jesus does. But in fact, Jesus uses his authority, not to attack the law properly understood, but to go beyond it to the values which the law aimed to protect. The following table tries to analyse this:

| Law | Values |
| --- | --- |
| You shall not kill | Unwillingness to harm another, even in thought. Respect for the reputation of another. Love which forgives rather than insults. |
| You shall not commit adultery | Respect for others in their relationships, and the restraint this may demand, not only in action, but even in thought and desire. |
| You shall not swear falsely | Respect for the name of God and for truth, which makes an oath unnecessary. |
| An eye for an eye and a tooth for a tooth (that is, do not in revenge take more than your due). | Generosity, not clinging to one's rights, being prepared to share what one has. |
| You shall love your neighbour and hate your enemy. | Goodwill towards all men; love which knows no enemies, and is a reflection of the love God has for all men. |

> Examine this analysis and test it against the actual words of Jesus. Think
> about it and discuss it. Then try to say in your own words what you think
> Jesus is teaching here. Finally, write a short essay to show that in Jesus's
> opinion someone's inner dispositions are more important than mere
> outward observance of the law.

In fact there is nothing new, and certainly nothing anti-Jewish, in the
teachings of Jesus here. Everything he says can be matched from the
finest passages in the writings of the Jewish rabbis. But gathering
them together like this enables Matthew to show the power of Jesus's
moral teaching, and how he reveals the true meaning of the moral
law by asking of his followers much more than outward correctness.

### Real religion (6:1–24)

Continuing this emphasis on the importance of motive, Matthew
then quotes Jesus concerning three practices: alms-giving, personal
prayer and fasting. He warns against doing these things merely in
order to show off. Concerning prayer, Matthew inserts Jesus's
warning against thinking that the more prayers one says, the better
one prays. He also includes the prayer Jesus taught his disciples,
which already by Matthew's day had become *the* prayer of the
Christian community. (Incidentally, when they said it in public, they
felt the need to conclude it, as they concluded most prayers, by
something like the 'Glory be to the Father' ... what was called a
*doxology*, or a praising-prayer. So they added: *For thine is the kingdom,
the power and the glory, for ever and ever. Amen.* So habitual was this
ending quite early in the Church's history that it is found included in
some early copies of Matthew's gospel; but not in all, so it is generally
thought to be a later addition. It is still often used when the Lord's
Prayer is said.)

The verse *forgive us our debts as we also forgive our debtors* is repeated
and expanded by Matthew in a kind of postscript (v. 14). There is a
strong emphasis in Matthew's gospel on forgiveness (see Matt. 18:21
and 18:23–35).

This section on alms-giving, prayer and fasting concludes with
three mini-parables (6:19–21 and 6:22–3). The reference to the *moth*
that can attack treasure is understandable if one remembers that
riches often lay (as among some African peoples today) in the
possession of beautiful materials and beautiful clothes. The second
parable stresses the importance of 'seeing right' in the conduct of
one's life. *Mammon* in the third parable means *money*. Jesus is not
saying that it is wrong to have money, but that one cannot *serve* God
and money; that is, if money rules the life of a man, he cannot be a
disciple.

## True wisdom (6:25–34)

This leads naturally to a very well-known saying of Jesus about the disciple's attitude to material things. Its setting is surely the Galilean countryside in spring, when the air is full of birdsong and the fields covered with wild flowers, which spring up quickly when the winter passes and wither as quickly in the heat of the summer sun. Among them is a large red anemone-like flower known today as the *lily of the fields*. By the poetry of his language Jesus shows his sensitivity to the beauty of nature. The moral of the passage is, as a modern writer expresses it, *You are more important than the clothes you wear*. The disciple is not anxious and worried about material things, but trusts that if he puts first *the kingdom of God and its righteousness* his basic needs will be cared for.

X is a married man with two children. X's brother-in-law has a serious nervous breakdown. X takes time off work to look after his brother-in-law, who relies heavily on him, and to help his sister and their children, who cannot cope alone with the situation.

At the end of his period of leave, X goes to his employer and asks for an extension, as his brother-in-law is still ill. His employer says: 'Sorry – we cannot give you any longer. Either you come back to work on Monday or we sign you off for good. After all, he isn't even your own brother . . .' X, with the consent of his wife, stays with his brother-in-law and loses his job at a time of high unemployment. (*Note*: this is a true story.)

Would you say that X has taken seriously the words of Jesus and has been let down?

## Conclusion (7:1–29)

Finally there is a cluster of apparently unrelated sayings through which can be heard a note of relaxed humour in the way they are expressed. There is humour in the picture of someone trying to take a *speck* out of someone else's eye when there is a *log* in his own eye; in the picture of pearls being thrown into a pig-sty for pigs to admire; of wolves dressed up in sheepskins; of people trying to pick grapes from thorn-trees, or figs from thistles. The lesson of each saying is not difficult to grasp.

And the *Sermon* concludes with one final parable. It is best understood in the context of the climate of Palestine. A great part of the year is dry, but when the rains come they are heavy, and the water races down the hillsides. A house newly-built on rock would not be affected by the floodwater, but a house built on sand would risk having its foundations washed away. Jesus's teaching, the parable implies, is the rock which gives a sure foundation to a man's life.

Some of the themes introduced in the Sermon on the Mount are expanded elsewhere in Matthew's gospel.

Extending your evidence by looking up the references given below, write an essay on: The teaching of Jesus, according to Matthew, on
(a) forgiveness (see Matt. 6:12–15; 18:21; and 18:23–35)
(b) wealth and material possessions (see Matt. 7:24; 7:25–33; and 19:16–30)
(c) prayer (see Matt. 6:5–13; 7:7–11)

# 12 The community of believers, sign of the kingdom (Matt. 10 and 18)

Two of the five divisions of Matthew's gospel (see p.113) contain instructions given by Jesus to his followers and their leaders. Mark has similar passages, but Matthew expands them, gives them prominence, and sometimes applies them directly to the problems of the Christian church of his day. Matthew seems particularly aware of the problems of leadership in the church.

Chapter 10 opens with the calling of the twelve apostles. It is derived mainly from Mark 6:7–13. Again it is useful to compare Matthew with his source.

**Mark 6:7–13**

And he called to him the twelve, and began to send them out two by two, and gave them authority over the unclean spirits

He charged them to take nothing for their journey except a staff; no bread, no money in their belts; but to wear sandals, and not to put on two tunics.

And he said to them: 'Whenever you enter a house stay there until you leave the place.

**Matt 10:1–16**

And he called to him his twelve disciples and gave them authority over unclean spirits, to cast them out and to heal every disease and every infirmity.
(Matthew here gives the list of the twelve, which Mark had already given in Chapter 3)
These twelve Jesus sent out, charging them: 'Go nowhere among the gentiles, and enter no town of the Samaritans, but go rather to the lost sheep of the house of Israel. And preach as you go, saying: The kingdom of God is at hand. Heal the sick, raise the dead, cleanse lepers and cast out demons. You received without pay, give without pay.'
Take no gold, nor silver, nor copper in your belts, no bag for your journey, nor two tunics, nor sandals, nor a staff. For the labourer deserves his food.
And whatever town or village you enter, find out who is worthy in it, and stay with him until you depart. As you enter the house, salute it. And if the house is worthy, let your peace come upon it; but if it is not worthy, let your peace return to you.

| **Mark 6:7–13** | **Matt 10:1–16** |
|---|---|
| And if any place will not receive you and they refuse to hear you, shake off the dust that is on your feet as a testimony against them. | And if anyone will not receive you or listen to your words, shake off the dust from your feet as you leave that house or town. Truly I say to you, it shall be more tolerable on the day of judgement for Sodom and Gomorrah than for that town. |

Again, in contrast to the miracle-stories, Matthew's version is the longer. The most notable addition is the passage beginning: *Go nowhere among the gentiles* ... It is amazing to find this in a gospel generally thought to be written for the church at Antioch, where gentiles were first received as converts. One explanation may be that Matthew took it from the early collection of *Sayings* which appears to have been originally written in Hebrew and therefore the property of a Jewish-Christian church. Another explanation is offered by those who point out that in Matthew's gospel this occurs before the episode of the Syro-Phoenician woman (Matt. 15.21–28) which opened the mission of Jesus to the gentiles.

Apart from this lengthy addition, there are details which suggest that the church has grown and developed by the time Matthew is writing. Apparently there are by now little communities established which would be prepared to welcome a wandering preacher and house and feed him, considering that *the labourer deserves his food.* The apostles could expect to find in any town or village *worthy* people, Christians presumably, with whom they could stay. There is an established form of greeting (to this day, Christian ministers entering a house often say: Peace be to this house.) The apostles are not automatically listened to, but to reject their message is regarded as a misdeed deserving of extreme punishment (according to Genesis 19:24, Sodom and Gomorrah were destroyed by fire for their wickedness).

There are echoes of the eight beatitudes in these instructions. The apostles must be generous, poor in spirit and detached from earthly possessions (10:9). They are to be peace-makers (10:13), and if they are not made welcome, they are not to retaliate, but peacefully leave the house or town, shaking the dust from their feet, but leaving any retribution to the end-judgement (as compared with Mark, where the shaking off of dust is *a testimony against them*). They are to be *meek,* gentle as sheep among wolves, humble and willing to accept persecution, fearless and confident nevertheless. The words *you are of more value than many sparrows* (10:31) echo the *lilies of the field* (6.28). In a word, the apostles must not only preach the gospel, they must live it.

### Church leadership (18:15–20)
The sayings gathered together in the first ten verses of Matthew, chapter 18 reproduce passages from Mark (Mk 10:15; 9:37; 9:42–8)

and are about discipleship in general. But Matthew is specially concerned for those in leadership positions. This soon becomes apparent. You have already noted (p. 21) the ending he gives to the parable of the lost sheep, applying it to the task of the *shepherd*. Verses 16–20 deal with a problem which (as we know from the letters of Paul) soon made itself felt in the early Church. Their community was a community held together by love in the following of Christ. What were they to do if one of their members misbehaved? Matthew gives them a pattern of behaviour (18:15–17) which takes for granted a certain degree of organisation in the community. The use of words like *the church*, which would not have been appropriate in Jesus's own lifetime, shows clearly that Matthew is here adapting the words of Jesus to the Christians of his generation. The expression *as a gentile and a tax-collector* suggests that this was written primarily for a Jewish-Christian community.

Examine the advice given in 18:15–20 about how to deal with an offender. What do you think about it? Could it apply to any other society?

## Forgiveness (Matt. 18:21,22)
There is a great deal in this chapter about the community of believers which came to be known as *the church* (from a Greek word meaning an *assembly*, a *gathering*). It had by now some sort of organisation. But essentially it was a community of friends, of brothers and sisters, of *little ones* (v. 4). Their only power was the power of prayer, their only support was their faith in the presence with them of the risen Christ. Because they remain ordinary men and women, they will quarrel. But they are called by Jesus to live in a relationship of love. So they will have to forgive each other. Peter feels that there must be a limit to this. How many times does one have to forgive? Up to seven times? (He obviously thought he was being generous.) The reply of Jesus means that there is no limit. It is not something that you calculate about. And to drive the lesson home he tells a story . . .

### The parable of the Unforgiving Servant (Matt. 18:23–35)
A *denarius* was the daily wage of a labourer. A *talent* was the highest unit of currency of the Near East at that time, and *ten thousand* was the highest number used in reckoning (as the billion is with us). No higher sum could therefore be imagined than ten thousand talents. The contrast between the enormous sum owed by the servant to the king, and the relatively tiny sum owed by his fellow-servant, is the point of the parable. God forgives so much: should his followers not forgive each other? Peter is answered.

# 13  The parables of the kingdom
(Matt. 13, 20 and 25)

The Parable of the Two Debtors answered Peter's question more powerfully than mere argument could have done. The parables of Jesus occupy an important place in the *Sayings of Jesus* which have been handed down.

The parables (see see p. 42) are comparisons in story form, drawing upon the everyday life of Palestine and on events which were in the news. They were probably spoken by Jesus on the spur of the moment when he found himself in argument, trying to convey to his hearers a truth which they would find new (and therefore difficult to understand) or disturbing (and therefore difficult to accept). The advantage of the parable was that without argument it led the hearer to see for himself what the truth of the matter must be.

Because the parables were stories, they were easily remembered. Sometimes they were still remembered when the occasion which gave rise to them was forgotten. Then it is not always easy – sometimes it is impossible – to know what meaning they would have had in their original context, since the situation was the key to their meaning. Separated from their context they can be quite puzzling. Because it was Jesus who had told them, they were still remembered and repeated even when the reason why he told them had been forgotten. The next step was to see other meanings in them, other ways in which they can apply to life.

So when the question is asked today: *What is the meaning of this parable?* the question can mean any one of three things.

A. What was the point of the parable when Jesus first told it? (The answer will depend on what can be known or deduced about the circumstances in which it was spoken by Jesus.)

B. What point was being made by the gospel-writer when he inserted this parable into his gospel? (The answer will depend on the context of the parable in that particular gospel, and our knowledge of the situation for which the gospel was written.)

C. What does the parable say to me in my life at this moment?

This book will study the parables in the light of questions A and B only. Question C is a wholly private question; it is therefore left to each one of you to answer it to yourself if you wish.

You already know enough about two particular parables to make an attempt at questions A and B for yourselves.
   The parables are: *The Lost Sheep* (Lk. 15:3–7 and Matt. 18:12–14) and *The Sower* (Mk 4. 3–20 and Matt. 13:3–23)
   Look them up and have a go.

In the Parable of the Sower, did you notice one significant alteration which Matthew has made to Mark's text? (see Matt. 13:10–17) In both gospels the 'explanation' shifts the emphasis from the seed to the soil. In the context of Mark's church and of Matthew's, it is used to explain why everyone did not receive the gospel. Both contrast the crowd who did not understand with the disciples who did. But the comparison is much stronger in Matthew, as he quotes at length from the prophecy of Isaiah to suggest that, in the case of those who do not receive the word, it is more a case of *will not* than of *can not*.

**The Parable of the Weeds** (Matt. 13:24–30) This parable is told only by Matthew. The Greek word here translated *weed* does not mean any weed, but one particular weed (generally translated *darnel* or *tare*) which looks very much like wheat in the early stages of its growth. With relation to this parable, Question A is difficult to answer. There is no clue to the precise occasion when Jesus spoke this parable. It seems to fit an occasion like Luke 9:51–6, or to illustrate Jesus's teaching in Matt. 7:1, *Judge not* . . . . The emphasis in the story itself is certainly on patience, on not judging between people, not dividing them into good and bad (is it all that easy to see which is which?).

Question B is helped by the *explanation* – a later application of the parable which turns it into an allegory (see p. 42) and shifts the emphasis to the final judgement. Remembering the situation of the church in Antioch, now officially separated from the Jewish community, some think that for Matthew and his readers the wheat may have represented the new Israel (the true Israel) and the weeds the old (unfaithful) Israel, which were to exist side by side until the day of judgement.

The Parables of the *Mustard Seed* and of the *Leaven* are taken almost word for word from Mark. The twin Parables of the *Treasure in the Field* and the *Pearl* are not difficult to interpret. The emphasis is on the value of what is found and the joy of the finder. In the parable which follows, the mixed bag of fish in the *drag-net* is an image of any believing community, and its lesson is clear.

**The Parable of the Vineyard** in Matt. 20:1–16 is another parable told only by Matthew. Its setting belongs to the Palestine of Jesus's day. The proper care of a vineyard demands a great deal of labour at certain times of the year (e.g. for the grape harvest) and casual labour would then be used. So the owner goes out to look for the unemployed hanging around in the market-place. The denarius which he offers was the normal wage of an unskilled worker. The story has a surprise ending: at the end of the day all receive the same wage, no matter how long they have worked. Those who have worked all day feel themselves unjustly treated. The punch-line comes at the end. *Do you begrudge my generosity?*

We have no clue to the situation in which Jesus told this story, but its meaning, following the clue in the punch-line, fits in well with his general message. The owner of the vineyard obviously represents God (see p. 82). He is characterised, says Jesus, by his generosity, by his superabundant love (compare Matt. 6:45–8). His gifts to his children are not governed by arithmetic, any more than their love for and forgiveness of each other must be governed by arithmetic (Matt. 18:21–2). Men tend to judge God by their own standards, and find it difficult to believe in his love. Jesus tells this startling story to open the hearts of his hearers to the love of the Father whom he has come to reveal.

In the context of Matthew's church a different application has been suggested by the addition of a sentence: *So the last will be first and the first last.* This seizes upon a detail in verse 8, and makes it the conclusion of the parable, changing its emphasis and obscuring its original message. Given Matthew's preoccupation with the new Israel and the old Israel, some think that the labourers who were taken on at the last moment had come to represent, for Matthew, the gentiles; and that those who grumbled represent the faithful Jews who were not too pleased to see gentiles admitted to the Christian community at this point in history.

In Chapter 25 are three other parables which are told only by Matthew.

**The Parable of the Ten Maidens** (Matt. 25:1–13) The situation described in this parable is familiar to those who know Jewish marriage customs. After the wedding day had been spent in dancing and other festivities, the wedding feast took place at night in the house of the bridegroom. The bride was taken there first in a torchlight procession. The women who had escorted her waited until they were told that the bridegroom was on his way, then they went out to meet him and accompanied him and his friends back to the house.

A glance at chapter 24 shows the context in which Matthew places this parable. Chapter 24 is similar to Mark 13 (look back to p. 85 onwards). Can you see the connection?

**The Parable of the Talents** (Matt. 25:14–30) This parable has the same kind of surprise ending as that of the labourers in the vineyard. The man who handed back his talent unused had at least kept it safe. But the master blamed him. It is not clear why, nor what situation in Jesus's life or in Matthew's church the parable is addressed to.

One theory with regard to the original point of the parable is based on the sentence: *You ought to have invested my money with the bankers, and at my coming I should have received what was my own with interest.* The law forbade a Jew to take interest from another Jew, but he could from a gentile. It has been suggested that this parable was originally aimed at the scribes who, entrusted with God's Law, hedged it around with precautions and would have no contact with gentiles in case they should be defiled.

In Luke's version of the parable (which is probably an earlier one) each of the three men is given an equal amount of money. Matthew may have altered this to give the parable another application for his church, namely, that everyone must make the most of any gift he has been given. It then appears as an illustration of the maxim *For to everyone that has, to him shall be given, and he will have in abundance; but from him who has not, even what he has will be taken away* – a maxim quoted by Matthew in 13:12.

**The Parable of the Judgement** (Matt. 25:31–46) The image used in this parable of separating sheep from goats is derived from a scene still familiar in the Near East. Goats and sheep are pastured together during the day, but in the evening they are separated, as the goats need shelter for the night, whereas the sheep are hardier and can stay out of doors.

This is the best-known of Jesus's parables. Matthew makes no comment (it speaks for itself); he simply quotes it as the climax of Jesus's teaching.

> (a) Using as your reference the parables found in Matthew's gospel, show how closely they are rooted in the geography and customs of the Palestine of Jesus's day.
>
> (b) On p. 122 it was suggested that Jesus used parables when he wanted to convey a truth which was either new and therefore difficult to grasp, or disturbing and therefore difficult to accept. For each of the parables reviewed in this chapter, state in your own words the truth it teaches, and say whether this truth would have been new, or disturbing (or both) to Jesus's hearers and Matthew's readers.

*Note on the sufferings and death of Jesus according to Matthew*

The account of the death of Jesus in Matt. 26 and 27 follows closely Mark's account in Mk 14 and 15. But there are minor differences, mainly additions. Study for yourselves the two accounts, make a note of the differences, and group them as follows:

A. Differences concerning the apostles, especially Peter.
B. Differences concerning Judas
C. Differences concerning the leaders of the Jews.
D. Differences concerning Pilate.

Do you think these differences significantly alter the general picture?

# 14  The birth and childhood of Jesus according to Matthew (Matt. 1 and 2)

The evidence of Church documents such as the *Letters* of Paul, the Gospel of Mark, and the Acts of the Apostles, suggests that whenever the gospel of Jesus was preached, it began with the baptism of Jesus by John in the Jordan. Matthew's gospel could easily have begun, therefore, with 3:1 (*In those days came John the Baptist* ...) In fact Matthew has prefaced this with a little collection of stories relating to the birth and childhood of Jesus.

The public life of every great man gives rise to an interest in and a curiosity about his earlier experiences. Where did he come from? What were his family roots? When did his parents first realise, for example, that he was musical? ... The few available facts may be surrounded by a certain amount of romanticising.

Certainly some such curiosity surrounded after a while the earlier life of Jesus. As time went on a number of stories, some of them very fanciful, were told about his earlier days. (You may have heard the one, written up into a poem by Hilaire Belloc, telling how he was playing with other children modelling birds out of clay, when those which the boy Jesus had modelled spread their wings and flew away.) Matthew's *infancy narratives*, as they are called, are very different from these collections of pretty stories. Wherever he may have found the stories he uses in chapters 1 and 2, Matthew is not merely collecting echoes, true or invented, of Jesus's childhood. His purpose is far more serious.

To understand these chapters rightly, it is important to remember once again what a *gospel* is. The essence of the *good news* which is being proclaimed is in the death and resurrection of Jesus which revealed him as Lord and Saviour. The gospels were 'written backwards', not in the sense that the last chapters were written first (though in a way they were, since the Passion had been told so often that the evangelist almost found his narrative ready-made), but in the sense that all the events of Jesus's life were told in the light of what was revealed at the end. They are told so that the reader may see, through them, who Jesus was finally shown to be for men. This is true even of the infancy narratives. Chapters 1 and 2 may in fact have been written last, and then pre-fixed to the gospel as a kind of foreword. It is certain that, by selecting these particular stories and by the way he tells them, Matthew underlines some of the most important things he wants to say about Jesus throughout his gospel. They are not dictated by curiosity, but are part of his message.

## The genealogy

Matthew begins with *the book of the genealogy of Jesus Christ*. Genealogies (or lists of ancestors) were important among the Jews. Being descended from this or that famous person could entitle you to certain political or religious privileges. These genealogies were not like the family trees which you could draw up for yourselves if you were able to trace your grandparents on both sides, their parents (your great-grandparents), your great-great-grandparents and so on. For centuries the Jews had relied on memory rather than on written records (though by Jesus's time these genealogies were written down). So they were content to remember the best-known names, and did not worry if they skipped a generation here and there. And because a man's genealogy might be drawn up for different purposes (for example, political or religious) they could choose, for example, which grandparent to go through. This meant that a man could have more than one genealogy, according to the purpose of each.

As Matthew himself points out (1:17) the genealogy provided for Jesus here is a very tidy one. It is built around three great dates in the history of the Jewish people: the time of Abraham (around 1800 BC); the time of David (around 1000 BC) and the time of the Babylonian Exile (586 BC). These dates divide the time since Abraham into three unequal periods, but ancestors' names have been chosen so as to give fourteen generations in each period. The fact that Matthew points this out may mean that it is a kind of code.

*Crack the code*
Here are your clues: The Hebrew written language had no numerals (like our 1, 2, 3 . . .) When they wanted to write down a number, they used letters, so each letter in the alphabet was made to stand for a certain number. For example, D = 4 and V = 6.

There were no vowels in Hebrew. So David's name would be written DVD.

Throughout Matthew's gospel the title 'Son of David' is used far more frequently of Jesus than it is in Mark. Why 14 + 14 + 14 in the genealogy?

Why then did Matthew not simply begin the list with *David*? Why go back to Abraham?

Abraham was not only the father of the Jewish race. He had also received from God the promise that through him and his descendants *all the nations of the earth* would be blessed (Gen. 22:18). Jesus had come, says Matthew, not only for the salvation of the Jews, but for all peoples; and in extending his mercy to all nations he was not being unfaithful to his Jewishness, but fulfilling it. This too is central to Matthew's message.

Look back over the gospel of Matthew, and note all the places where Jesus is shown as fulfilling the law, and where non-Jews are shown as children of Abraham.

Mark had begun his gospel by a statement of what he believes: the good news of *Jesus Christ the Son of God*. Matthew has established through the genealogy that Jesus was son of David and son of Abraham. He now goes on in his own way to declare him *Son of God*.

## The Birth of Jesus (Matt. 1:18–25)

He does this by telling how Jesus came to be born, and by attributing the conception of Jesus not to intercourse between Mary and Joseph her husband, but to a direct creative act of God. The text says: *When his mother Mary had been betrothed to Joseph, before they came together, she was found to be with child by the Holy Spirit . . .* (1:18)

A Jewish wedding took place in two stages: first came a formal exchange of consent before two witnesses (like our marriage ceremony) which made the couple husband and wife, though they still kept apart and the young woman continued to live in her parents' house. Then after an interval – generally about a year – the bride was taken to the bridegroom's house (compare the Parable of the Ten Maidens, p. 124) and the marriage was completed. If a wife was found, on arrival at her husband's house, not to be a virgin, she could be accused of infidelity. The punishment for this in strict Jewish law was stoning. Joseph was prepared to take a kinder way and divorce Mary without public accusation and trial. But (like another Joseph in the Old Testament) he was helped by a dream to understand what was happening. He therefore took Mary as his wife and acknowledged the child as his own by giving him a name (Jesus = Saviour).

For many centuries Christians were united in taking literally the story of the *Virgin Birth* of Jesus. Today they are divided in their interpretation. The majority – particularly the Roman Catholic Church and the Eastern Church – continue to see in it a literal breaking through of God into this world, a quickening of life through the power of God's Spirit, to begin a new creation with the life, death and resurrection of Jesus. Others see no need of such direct action to fulfil God's purpose in a world where the life-giving power of God normally acts through the world he has created and is present in every birth; so they interpret this story as Matthew's way of saying as strongly as he can that only God can bring salvation to men. All agree that this is what is stated, either by the event or by the story: God alone is the source of salvation, says Matthew, and if Jesus is saviour it is because he is the Son of God.

### Wise Men from the East (2:1–12)

The story of the Wise Men (who said there were three?) is full of meaning. As *wise men from the East* they represent the *all nations* who, says Matthew throughout his gospel, are to come to Jesus. Being pagans, they are drawn to him first by a sign in nature; but the Jews, with their special revelation in Scripture of the plan of God, have a special part to play in bringing them to Jesus. The wise men offer him gifts of gold, frankincense and myrrh – a detail relating to the prophecy in which Isaiah foretells Jerusalem's future glory:

Arise, shine, for your light has come,
and the glory of the Lord has risen upon you ...
Nations shall come to your light
and kings to the brightness of your rising ...
The wealth of nations shall come,
all those from Sheba have come.
They shall bring gold and frankincense
and shall proclaim the praise of the Lord. (Is. 60:1–6)

# Herod (2:13–18)

Intertwined with the story of the wise men is the story of the cruelty of Herod and the massacre of the children. This story too has a strong Old Testament reference: it recalls Pharaoh's attempt (Exodus 1:8 – 2:10) to wipe out the early Hebrews by ordering all their male children to be killed off at birth, and how Moses was saved from this massacre to become the saviour of his people and lead them out of Egypt.

This constant link with the Old Testament is a feature of these first two chapters. Four times passages from the Old Testament are quoted or referred to. They are important clues to Matthew's meaning. It is not that something which he is saying happens to remind him of an Old Testament verse, which he then quotes. It is rather that, as a good Jew, he has meditated deeply on God's dealings with his people throughout their history, and has been helped by this to see how all God's purposes, and his people's destiny, are fulfilled in Jesus.

Below are the quotations used by Matthew in this chapter, and notes on the original context of each. Look at each in the context in which Matthew places it, and say in your own words what connection Matthew sees between it and Jesus:

(a) Matt. 1:23: *Behold a virgin shall conceive and bear a son, and his name shall be called Emmanuel.* These words, from Isaiah 7.14, refer to the state of affairs in Jerusalem seven centuries before Christ. The Assyrian armies threatened to overrun the whole of the Near East. Ahaz, king of Jerusalem, is terrified. This is the end. His own armies are powerless against the heavy and better-armed forces of the Assyrians. He and his people will be overcome, and since he has no son to take up the fight after him, the history of the people of God is finished. He is tempted to abandon his usual allies, Israel and Damascus, and go over to the side of Assyria. Isaiah reproaches him for relying on tricky alliances rather than on the promises of God, and declares that a child will be born through whom David's line will be preserved, and that God *is* with us, on our side. (The prophecy came true in that Ahaz did have a son and successor, Hezekiah, who successfully defended Jerusalem against the Assyrian general Sennacherib in 701 BC.)

(b) Matt. 2:6: *And you, Bethlehem . . .* (from Micah 5:2). This was written in the same political situation as Isaiah 7, and expresses the same longing for the birth of a better king, descendant of David (whose family was from Bethlehem) to carry God's promise to fulfilment.

(c) Matt. 2:15: *Out of Egypt I have called my son . . .* (from Hosea 11.1). The prophet is reproaching the people for abandoning the worship of God for that of pagan idols. Through him God reminds his people of how he has loved them in the past, and in particular when they were brought out of Egypt: *When Israel was a child I loved him, and out of Egypt I have called my son.*

(d) Matt. 2:18: *A voice in Ramah was heard . . .* (from Jeremiah 31:15). The original historical setting of this prophecy was the year 586, when the Babylonians conquered Jerusalem and deported all the leading families into Babylon so that they would not be able to cause any more trouble.

(cont'd)

They were first of all collected in a kind of transition camp at Ramah, a few miles north-east of Jerusalem. Now Rachel (Jacob's wife and Joseph's mother: see Genesis 29 onwards) was buried in Ramah. In the passage quoted she represents all the inhabitants of that area weeping for the fall of Jerusalem.

But the passage in Jeremiah is not all gloom. It goes on:

Thus says the Lord:
  Keep your voice from weeping
  and your eyes from tears . . .
There is hope for your future, says the Lord,
  and your children shall come back to their own country.
For the Lord has created a new thing on the earth . . .

(e)  Matt. 2:3: *He shall be called a Nazarene.* No sure explanation has been found for this quotation, which does not occur anywhere in the Old Testament.

If you have worked out the way Matthew applies each of these to his message about Jesus, you will have illustrated one of the ways in which he shows Jesus as fulfilling the promises of God to his people Israel.

This chapter has asked what these *infancy narratives* mean, why Matthew gathers them and weaves them together to make of them the prologue to his gospel. They have become for Christians part of the 'Christmas story'. Curiosity asks: Where do they come from? Are they memories of real events? or invented stories? . . . Again Christians are divided in their answers. On the one hand these stories fit well into their historical context: Eastern countries like Persia, for example, were known for their *wise men*, famed among other things for their study of the stars; and Herod is notorious for his readiness to murder anyone – including members of his own family – who got in his way. On the other hand, if such tremendous events did mark the birth of Jesus, it is strange that they were forgotten so quickly that his friends and neighbours can comment on the 'ordinariness' of his life before his baptism by John (Matt. 13:54–6). We know that the Jews were accustomed to make up stories in their preaching so as to bring out the meaning of passages in Scripture: and some think that these stories may have come into the Christian community through preaching in a similar way. In any case, because of what Matthew says through them, they are very much part of his message about Jesus the Christ – very much part of his gospel.

Illustrate the last sentence by showing how Matthew in these two chapters declares:
(a)  that Jesus is the new Moses;
(b)  that Jesus is the new David;
(c)  that Jesus brings the sacred history of his people to fulfilment;
(d)  that through Jesus all men are called to know God.

# 15 What is the good news according to Matthew?

*The kingdom of heaven is at hand* (Matt. 4:17) ... Go therefore and *make disciples of all nations* ... *and lo, I am with you always to the close of the age* ... (Matt. 28:18–20). These words, taken from the beginning of the gospel and from its last paragraph, summarise the good news according to Matthew.

*The kingdom of heaven is at hand.* What was meant by the phrase *kingdom of heaven* which Matthew uses so often? (Luke was to say: *the kingdom of God*, which means the same thing. But the Jews avoided the name of God out of reverence. Matthew's Christians were, many of them, Jewish converts. So Matthew respects this, and speaks always of the kingdom of *heaven*.)

The Jews of Jesus's day believed that God was king of all ages and of all men, but that his kingship was only fully recognised in Israel. But they looked forward to a day when God would openly show himself as Ruler of all. He would, on that day, free his people from slavery and bring all nations to recognise his power and his will, establishing justice everywhere. Christians – and Matthew among them – believed two things about this kingdom. They believed that in one sense it had come in Jesus. Those who followed him, Jews or gentiles, felt themselves to be free people, happy because they knew that they were loved by God and that Jesus was still with them, and living in a fellowship of love, so that among themselves there was no injustice or oppression. They would have described this as living in the kingdom of God. But in another sense they believed that the kingdom was still to come. Jesus's life had contained many signs of the presence of God's kingdom, particularly in the healings he performed. But it was a suffering life; he had returned now to his Father, and would come again in the glory which belonged to him, to establish finally the kingdom of God on earth.

The first Christians expected this Second Coming of Christ to happen quite soon. (Maybe even Jesus himself had thought that it would.) By the time Matthew wrote his gospel, it was becoming clear that this was not to be. So discipleship, or living as Jesus had taught men to live, was becoming more important than waiting for him to come again.

Jesus lived, says Matthew, at the climax of his people's history. Born of an ancient Jewish family, tracing its origins back to David and even to Abraham, he was the complete Jew: all that the prophets of Israel had foretold was fulfilled in his life and his death. He respected the law. But he rejected a mere outward show of religion, and condemned the religious leaders of his day for their blindness to real spiritual values.

> *Note* Matthew suggests a much stronger opposition and conflict than did Mark between the scribes, Pharisees and priests on the one hand and Jesus on the other. Your comparison of the two versions of the Passion story must have shown how Matthew goes further than Mark in attributing Jesus's death to the Jews and showing the Romans in a favourable light. And there is nothing in Mark to compare with the fierceness of Matt. 23.

Jesus, says Matthew, did not destroy the law; he showed how perfect observance did not mean keeping hundreds of extra commandments; but it did mean tuning in to the interior attitudes which lay behind the law. He came as a great teacher, a new Moses, founder of a new Israel to replace the old. This new Israel would be open to all nations by faith.

*Make disciples* ... As in Mark's gospel, Jesus is shown by Matthew as drawing men to himself by the authority of his person and his teaching. From his followers he demands complete commitment. In Mark the emphasis was on the courage and constancy required of them in persecution. In Matthew the emphasis is on such qualities as gentleness, humility, peace-making, forgiveness, brotherly love. These are the social virtues, which enable men to live together in fellowship. The existence of a Christian fellowship (a 'church') is presupposed in Matthew's gospel. It has its leaders, a certain organisation, its code of behaviour, even its disciplinary powers. It comes together in prayer (both the *Our Father* in 6:9–13 and Jesus's words at the Last Supper in 26:26–28 read like the known formulas of public prayer).

*I am with you always* ... The greatest comfort of this little community among the pressures which surround it is its faith in the continued presence of Jesus the Lord. We have not yet looked at the last chapter, which treats of the resurrection. But in a sense the last chapter is superfluous; as in Mark, so in Matthew, the resurrection is presupposed throughout, and it is clear that the death of Jesus is by no means the end of the story. He is to come again – there is a strong emphasis on this in Matthew. But in the meantime he is not absent: where two or three are gathered in his name, he is in the midst of them (18:20); he is identified with all who suffer, so that to meet and give help to the poor and the suffering is to meet and to give help to him (10:42; 25:31–46); and he promises to be with those who take his yoke upon them (11:28–30) always *to the end of the age*. As the glory of God had dwelt with the old Israel in the form of a cloud or a pillar of fire, so Jesus the Lord would be present to and with the believing community as it tried to realise on earth God's kingdom of love, justice and peace.

# LUKE

## 16 The gospel according to Luke: the infancy narratives (Luke 1:5–2:52)

The author of the third synoptic gospel, according to authorities which go back to the second century, was Luke, a physician who accompanied Paul on some of his missionary journeys (see The Acts of the Apostles, and Paul's Letter to the Colossians 4:14).

His gospel opens with a formal dedication to a certain *Theophilus*.

> *Note* The name, which is Greek, means *loved by God* or *lover of God*. It was a well-known name, found in ancient papyri and inscriptions, and there is no reason to believe that he was not a real person. Luke also dedicates his second book, the Acts of the Apostles, to this same Theophilus.

The dedication is written in stylish Greek, and resembles the dedications with which Greek classical writers prefaced their works. Throughout the gospel (except for chapters 1 and 2) Luke writes smoothly and elegantly, in a way which suggests a very well-educated man.

The dedication makes it clear that Luke was not an eye-witness of the events of Jesus's life, but that he has taken the trouble to base his account on reliable sources. The most important of these are:

(a) the gospel of Mark
(b) the same book of *Sayings* which Matthew used
(c) a third source or sources, generally called L, which preserves many traditions that are neither in Matthew nor in Mark.

> *Stages in the making of the gospels*
> AD 27–30   Jesus proclaims the gospel
> AD 30–70   The Christian communities live out the gospel. They preach, they pray, they celebrate. Paul travels and spreads the gospel, and writes his letters. The disciples remember the events of Jesus's life and reflect on them in the light of the Old Testament and their daily lives.

(cont'd)

> AD 70–100  The written gospels emerge:
>   (a)  the gospel of Mark – in Rome, about AD 70
>   (b)  the gospel of Luke – in Syria?
>   (c)  the gospel of Matthew – in Antioch? (about AD 80–90)
>   (d)  the gospel of John – in Asia Minor? (about AD 100)

When Luke uses Mark he remains very true to his source, smoothing out Mark's rather rough style into something more elegant, but keeping its original sense. To discover the particular character of Luke's gospel, therefore, the special angle from which he sees the *good news,* it is more useful to concentrate on the passages which are found in Luke's gospel alone.

## Infancy narratives

Like Matthew, Luke begins his gospel with stories of the birth and childhood of Jesus. These stories are not the same as those in Matthew, and have obviously come from a different source. The style in which they are written (very different from the smooth Greek of the rest of the gospel) suggests that they come from a Hebrew source. They are not an insignificant preface, but very much part of the total gospel, for in them Luke states all the main ideas which he will develop later.

### The angel announces the birth of John (Lk. 1:5–25)

The story follows the pattern of several stories in the Old Testament where the birth of children who have a special part to play in God's plan is accompanied by signs of their future greatness. In particular, they are often shown to be 'god-sends' by being born of elderly and childless parents (e.g. Isaac in Gen. 18:9–15; 21:1–7; Samson in Judges 13:1–25; and Samuel in First Book of Samuel 1:1–20).

John's father was a priest, that is, a member of the Levite tribe who were consecrated to the service of the temple.

> *Note* The Levites were divided into twenty-four divisions, each of which served in the temple for one week every six months. There were four principal tasks to be performed: the offering of an animal killed and burnt to signify the giving back of all life to God; the offering of the meal, to acknowledge that all food, and therefore all life, comes from God; the care of the candlesticks in the Holy Place; and the offering of incense. Lots were drawn to decide who would do which. The offering of incense was considered the most privileged task, because for this the priest had to go into the inner sanctuary of the temple. No priest was allowed to do it for a second time until everyone else had had his turn, so it was a rare and precious occasion.

The angel announces not only that a son will be born to Elizabeth, but that his name must be *John* (= *gift of God*). Abstaining from wine and strong drink was a sign that he was to be specially consecrated to God (as both Samuel and Samson had been). As in Mark's gospel and Matthew's, so in Luke's, he is to be the *Elijah* who will prepare the way for the Messiah, not by some kind of re-incarnation, but because he will be filled with *the spirit and power of Elijah*. Zechariah cannot believe the message, and is immediately given a sign of God's power. Elizabeth says that God has *taken away her reproach among men* because the Jews regarded children as a sign of God's blessing, and to be childless was therefore a disgrace.

### The angel announces the birth of Jesus (Lk. 1:26–56)

The story of how Jesus was conceived is told differently by Luke and by Matthew. Both speak of Mary as a virgin, who conceives by the action of the Spirit and the power of God. But whereas Matthew tells the story from the point of view of Joseph, Luke tells it from the point of view of Mary – which led many early scholars to wonder whether Mary, directly or indirectly, might not have been one of the sources from which Luke obtained his information. Mary, like Zechariah, is given a sign, namely the pregnancy of her elderly cousin. Unlike Zechariah, she believes. Mary then sets out to visit her cousin Elizabeth, and is recognised by her as mother of the Messiah. Mary's song of praise (often called the *Magnificat* from the first word of the song in Latin) is made up of echoes of several hymns in the Old Testament, and resembles particularly the song of Hannah (1 Samuel 2:1–10). Since early Christian times many groups of Christians have used it in their official evening prayer.

### The birth of John and his father's song of praise (1:57–80)

In the story of John's birth great importance is given to his name. *John* means *gift of God*. Zechariah names him John because the angel had told him to. And his dumbness is cured. His song (known as the *Benedictus*, again from the first word of the Latin version) is a song of thanksgiving, joy and hope, acknowledging that the time has come when God will fulfil his age-old promise of salvation. (A *horn of salvation* means a *mighty saviour*: big horns were a sign of strength in an animal.) He prophesies that his son will prepare the way for the saviour.

John then disappears from the story (the reader is simply told that he *grew and became strong in spirit* and *was in the wilderness*) until he reappears in Chapter 3 preaching near the Jordan. Many have thought that during these years he may have joined a group of desert-dwellers called the *Essenes*.

*Note* The Essenes were a group of men who lived a kind of monastic existence on the shores of the Dead Sea. They had lost faith in the way the Jewish religion was being practised, and especially in its ceremonies. They turned their back on the temple and all it stood for, and went off to live their own way of life in the desert, waiting for the coming of the Teacher of Righteousness. Their monastery was sacked by the Roman armies after the destruction of Jerusalem, but before this happened they hid their library of writings (scrolls) in nearby caves, very difficult to get at. These scrolls (called the *Dead Sea Scrolls*) were accidentally discovered in 1947. They are important because (a) they tell us a great deal about the life and thought of this particular group and (b) among them were some of the earliest copies we possess of parts of the Old Testament, particularly the Book of Isaiah.

## The birth of Jesus and the angels' song of praise (2:1–20)

Luke takes care to set the birth of Jesus in the context of history. The information he gives, however, does not correspond with what we learn from other sources, nor even with Matt. 1:1, so it does not really enable us to date exactly the birth of Jesus.

---

*Historical note* Luke's information concerning the time when Jesus was born mentions a census of Judaea ordered by the Emperor Augustus, and taking place when Quirinius was governor of Syria. Luke also says (Lk. 1:5) that all these things happened *in the days of Herod, King of Judaea*.

Augustus was Emperor from 31 BC to AD 41. Quirinius, who was governor of Syria, was also in charge of Judaea from AD 6 to AD 26, when he was replaced by Pontius Pilate.

We know from other sources that in AD 6 Augustus caused a census to be taken in Judaea so that he could tax the inhabitants. It sounds as though this is the census Luke is referring to. But if so, it cannot be said to have taken place *in the days of Herod*, because Herod died in 4 BC.

Jesus cannot have been born both during the reign of Herod and when Quirinius had charge of Judaea.

---

All attempts to reconcile this discrepancy are unconvincing, and we can only conclude that Luke is giving, not a precise historical reference, but a memory in which two notable events – the death of Herod and the moment when the people of Judaea became subject to taxation – have been fused.

The demands of the census serve to explain why Joseph and Mary, who came from Nazareth, were in Bethlehem (city of David) for the birth. The *inn* was probably a caravanserai – an open quadrangle where camels and donkeys could be parked, surrounded by shelters for their owners (our motels are the nearest modern equivalent). Caves in the hillside were normally used to shelter animals, and would make at least a warm dry shelter for Mary and Joseph.

In the Palestine of Jesus's day certain occupations were considered defiling, and people who made their living that way were outcasts from society. Shepherds were in this category, (together with tanners and tax-collectors). But shepherds were the first to whom Jesus's birth was announced, and the first to worship him.

## Jesus is circumcised, and presented in the Temple

Every Jewish boy, a week after his birth, is circumcised as a sign that he belongs to the Jewish people. This is also a naming ceremony.

If he was also the first-born, he was considered as specially dedicated to God. In Jesus's day his parents then had to take him to the temple if possible, and buy him back, so to speak, by offering in his place either a lamb (if they were rich) or a pair of doves or pigeons (if they were poor). Mary and Joseph give the offering of the poor.

Luke sees a special significance in the first entry of Jesus into the temple, the building which for the Jews was the sign of God's presence. There he is recogised by two representatives of God's people, Simeon and Anna. Simeon's song of praise (known as the *Nunc Dimittis*) also became part of the official prayer of the Christian church, as the last prayer of the day.

Verse 40 reads like the ending of this section of the gospel. But Luke picks up his narrative again to give his readers the only tradition in the gospels concerning the boyhood of Jesus. At the age of twelve a Jewish boy became a man. He undertook to live by the Law from then on. In Jesus's time this meant that he was now bound to make the annual visit to the temple for the feast of Passover. Luke uses this story to underline the special vocation of Jesus.

In these first two chapters Luke has already expressed the main ideas which for him make up the *good news*.

The evidence for this is gathered and organised for you below. At the end of each section, complete for yourself the sentence which draws the conclusion:

(a) Jesus is called *saviour* (this is what the name *Jesus* means)
He is born of God's power, son of God (1:26–31).
Zechariah blesses God, who has *raised up a horn of salvation* in the house of David (1:69).
His son, John, is called to *give knowledge of salvation* by preparing the way for Jesus (1:77).
When Jesus is born the angels announce the birth of a *saviour who is Christ the Lord* (2:12).
Simeon, seeing the child carried into the Temple, now feels he can die in peace, because *mine eyes have seen thy salvation* (2:30).
Anna spoke of the child to all who were *looking for the redemption of Israel* (2:38).

**Conclusion**: The Jews had always thought of God as the one who *saves*. *I am the Lord thy God, who brought thee out of the land of Egypt and out of the house of bondage*. In these chapters Luke is saying that . . . .

(b) The child who is to be born (says the angel to Mary) will inherit *the throne of his father David* (1:32).
Mary recognises that this birth is *in remembrance of his mercy, as he spoke to our fathers, to Abraham and his posterity for ever* (1:54)
Zechariah realises that all was being done *as he spoke by the mouth of his holy prophets of old*, in a way *promised to our fathers*, in accordance *with his holy covenant, the oath he swore to our father Abraham* (1:70–73)

**Conclusion**: The salvation God holds out through Jesus fulfils . . . .

(c) Elizabeth and Zechariah would be looked down upon, because they were old and childless. Childlessness was a *reproach among men* (1:25)
Mary twice describes herself as the *handmaid* (or servant) *of the Lord* (1.38 and 1.48) and praises God who has regarded her *low estate*, whose mercy is on those who fear him, who has *scattered the proud*

(cont'd)

and raised up those who are of *low degree*, filling the *hungry* with good things and sending the rich away empty (1:48,50—53).
Jesus is born in the poverty of homelessness; his cradle is an animal's feeding-trough.
The shepherds, poor and despised, are the first to be informed of his birth and invited to meet him.
When Jesus is taken to be presented in the temple, the offering made for him is the offering of the poor.

**Conclusion**: Luke is saying that to be rich and powerful gives you no special claim to God's salvation. On the contrary, it is the gift of God's mercy, held out especially to . . . .

(d)  There are several references in these chapters to *Abraham*, in whom, says the Old Testament more than once, *all nations* shall be blessed. Salvation is *prepared in the presence of all peoples* (2:31)
The light which dawns with the coming of Jesus is for all *those who sit in darkness and the shadow of death* (1:79), a *light for revelation* to the gentiles as well as *glory to thy people Israel* (2:32).

**Conclusion**: God's salvation in Jesus is not just for . . . but also for . . . .

(e)  The angel promises Zechariah that John *will be filled with the Holy Spirit* even from his mother's womb (1:15).
To Mary the angel says: The *Holy Spirit* will come upon *you, and the power of the Most High will overshadow you* (1:35).
Elizabeth is *filled with the Holy Spirit* when Mary comes to her (1:42) and this enables her to recognise in Mary the mother of her Lord.
Zechariah, after John's birth, was *filled with the Holy Spirit* (1:67), and so was able to understand the meaning of what had happened.
The *Holy Spirit* was upon Simeon (2:25). It has been *revealed to him by the Spirit* that he should not see death before he had seen the Lord's Christ; and it was under the inspiration of the *Spirit* that he came into the temple and met the child Jesus (2:25—27).

**Conclusion**: Luke sees God as the power of love, at work in men's hearts, moving them to grasp God's plan and welcome Jesus. So he speaks of God as . . . .

(f)  The angel says to Zechariah: *You will have joy and gladness, and many will rejoice at his birth* (1:14).
When Mary visited Elizabeth, the baby in her womb *leaped for joy* (1:44).
When Elizabeth's son was born, her neighbours and her kinsfolk *rejoiced with her* (1:59).
Mary sang: *My soul magnifies the Lord, and my spirit rejoices* . . . (1:47).
The angels proclaimed the birth of Jesus as *news of great joy* (2:10).

**Conclusion**: For Luke the salvation which has come through Jesus is a source of . . . .

Finally, gather all these conclusions together, and try to write a mini-chapter to this book called: What is the *good news* according to Luke? (as far as you can gather from these first two chapters of Luke's gospel).

# 17 For all men and women

The old man Zechariah, in the first chapter of Luke's gospel, declared his belief in the dawning of the day of God's salvation, which will give *light to those who sit in darkness and the shadow of death*. Luke makes it clear that no category of persons is excluded from God's mercy.

## The Jews

He begins at home. Luke is clear that there is continuity between God's action in Jesus and his action in the history of his people, the Jews. Jesus is to sit on the *throne of his father David*, and *reign over the house of Jacob for ever* (1:32). Simeon recognised him as the *consolation of Israel*, the *glory of thy people Israel* (2:25,32). Throughout the gospel Jesus is shown preaching exclusively to the Jews and Samaritans. He omits a whole section of Mark's gospel (6:45–8:26) in which Mark shows Jesus going into gentile territory. Luke alone tells of Jesus weeping over Jerusalem (19:41–44). In his second volume, the Acts of the Apostles, Luke shows that, wherever the apostles went, they preached first to the Jews, the only then to the gentiles. Luke in his gospel seems to approve this order.

## Pagans

But gentiles are certainly not excluded.

*Note* It is thought that Luke himself may well have been a gentile Christian, or at least have been writing for a gentile-Christian church. Evidence for this is as follows:
(a) His 'Greek' background, suggested by the mastery which he shows over the Greek language.
(b) The dedication of his gospel to someone with a Greek name, and the way in which that dedication resembles the dedications of Greek classical writers.
(c) The way in which he translates Semitic words (that is, words in Hebrew or Aramaic) into their Greek equivalents. This is not always evident in the English translation: but examples are: 9:33 and 18:41, where he replaces Mark's word (which means *rabbi*) with a Greek word, *Master* or *Lord*; 6:15, where the Hebrew term for a 'daggerman' is replaced by the Greek *Zealot*; 10:25, where Mark's *scribe* (Mk 12:28) has become a *lawyer*; and 23:33, where the hill on which Jesus was crucified is simply *The Skull* as compared with Mark's *Golgotha*.
(d) His omission of passages in Mark dealing with things which particularly concern Jews, such as problems of ablutions in Mk 7:1–23, and the Mosaic law concerning divorce in Mk 10:2–12.

In any case, the infancy narratives, as has already been noted (p. 141), make it clear that God's salvation in Jesus is for all men. And in the genealogy which Luke composes for Jesus (3:23–38) he traces his ancestry back to *Adam*, father of the whole human race. A remarkable passage (found only in Luke) is 4:25–7, where Jesus compares his mission to that of Elijah and Elisha, both of whom had dealings with pagans. (Look up 1 Kings 17:8–16 and 2 Kings 5:1–19 for the incidents referred to.) In 13:24–9 the Jews are reminded that they will not be saved just because they are Jews, but that men will come from east and west, and from north and south, and sit at table in the kingdom of God. Comparing Luke 14:15–24 with the way Matthew tells the same story (22:1–10) draws attention to the repeated command of the master in Luke's version: *Go out into the streets and lanes of the city* ... (v. 21) *Go out to the highways and hedges* ... (v. 23). Luke may have intended those who came from the streets and lanes of the city to represent the Jews, and those who came from further afield (the highways and hedges) to stand for the gentiles. Jews and then gentiles – in that order.

## Samaritans

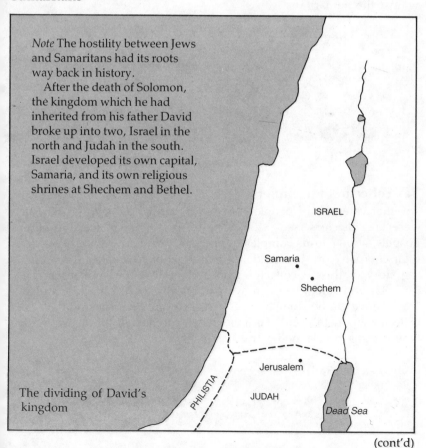

*Note* The hostility between Jews and Samaritans had its roots way back in history.

After the death of Solomon, the kingdom which he had inherited from his father David broke up into two, Israel in the north and Judah in the south. Israel developed its own capital, Samaria, and its own religious shrines at Shechem and Bethel.

ISRAEL

Samaria

Shechem

Jerusalem

PHILISTIA

JUDAH

Dead Sea

The dividing of David's kingdom

(cont'd)

When the invading armies came from the Mesopotamian plains from the eighth century BC to the sixth century BC, the northern kingdom was the first to fall. When finally the southern kingdom fell with the sacking of Jerusalem in 586 BC, its chief families were deported into Babylon. This had not happened to the same extent in the north. The people of Samaria had lived side by side with their conquerors for over two centuries, and after a while intermarried with them.

Babylon was conquered by the Persians, and their leader Cyrus allowed the Jews in Babylon to go home. They set to work to rebuild Jerusalem and the temple, but got no cooperation from the Samaritans, who had set up a shrine of their own on Mount Gerizim. The newly-returned Jews despised the Samaritans also because they were of mixed blood – not pure Jews. In the second century BC, to make it worse, the Samaritans had taken sides with the Syrians in the Syrian attack on the Jews. And the Jews had retaliated in 125 BC by burning down the temple which the Samaritans had built on Mount Gerizim.

All this had created deep enmity between the peoples of the two provinces, Judaea and Samaria.

Jesus seems to have been remarkably free from his people's prejudice against the Samaritans.

(a) Compare Matt. 10:5–8 and Lk. 9:51–6. What difference do you perceive regarding Jesus's attitude to the Samaritans?
(b) Look up Lk. 10:25–37. What significance is there in the fact that it was a Samaritan who came to the rescue? (This parable is found only in Luke's gospel.)
(c) Look up Luke 17:11–19 (also told only by Luke). What is the point of the sentence *Now he was a Samaritan*? (v. 17)
(d) Write a short essay on: The attitude of Jesus towards the Samaritans, as shown in the gospel of Luke.

## Tax-collectors and sinners

Another category of people generally regarded as beyond the pale were tax-collectors (see p. 34). The gospel of Luke, like the other gospels, shows Jesus completely open to them and even seeking out their company, to the scandal of many people. He takes from Mark the story of the tax-collector who became a follower of Jesus (Lk. 5:27–32) and refers to them sympathetically in 7:29 and 34; and in 15:1. Above all, he alone has the Parable of the Pharisee and the Tax-collector (18:9–14), and the incident of Zacchaeus, the tax-collector whom Jesus proclaimed a true *son of Abraham* (19:1–10).

(a) Read the Parable of the Pharisee and the Tax-collector. What is its point?
(b) Study 19:1–10. Comment, in the light of this story, on the words *salvation is come to this house*.

Tax-collectors are always mentioned in the same breath as *sinners*. Three times in Luke's gospel Jesus is reproached for eating with tax-collectors and sinners. His defence on the first occasion was to declare that his mission was precisely to show God's mercy to the sinner: *I have not come to call the righteous, but sinners to repentance* (5:32). The third occasion (15:1) introduces three parables, two of which are told only by Luke.

**The Parable of the Lost Sheep** (15:3–7) has already been referred to on p. 21. Luke's version emphasises the concern of the shepherd for his sheep, his tenderness towards the lost one, and above all his joy when it is found.

**The Parable of the Lost Coin** (15:8–10) is a woman's version of the parable of the lost sheep. The women who listened to Jesus would not have experienced the anxiety of the shepherd, but more than one of them would know what it was like to drop one small (but valuable) coin on the earthen floor of a dimly-lit Palestinian house (which would have only a low door and probably no window) and to have to search for it with the aid of a candle and a broom of palm-twigs. Her search would have been frantic if the coin she had lost was one of those which she wore round her head-dress, for in that case it would represent her dowry. Once again in this parable the emphasis is on the search, above all on the joy of finding.

**The Parable of the Prodigal Son** is the most powerful (15:11–32). It is a real-life story, with many details which ring true to Palestinian life at the time. The younger son asks for his share of the property: with one elder brother, he (the younger) would be entitled to one-third. He could either inherit this at his father's death, or receive the capital by gift during his father's lifetime. To have to look after pigs in order to stay alive would be, for a Jew, to be reduced to the absolute limit. The details of his welcome home indicate a great deal: the *best robe* was given only to a highly-honoured guest; the *ring* was a sign of authority; and the *shoes* the sign of a free man (slaves went barefoot); and in a country where meat was rarely eaten, a fatted calf was killed on very special occasions, and meant a feast for the whole household including the servants.

The word *prodigal* means very generous, or spendthrift. The parable has come to be known as the parable of the prodigal son, because of the way he squandered his money. But many people think that *the prodigal father* would be a better title, since the father is so generous towards his son. The parable describes what God is like, his goodness, his mercy, his overflowing love. The emphasis is again on joy at the return of the lost one.

The second half of the parable is a lesson to those who had criticised Jesus for his conduct towards sinners. The elder son represented the same spirit of mean criticism, the same inability to rejoice in the care of God for sinners.

Finally, Jesus not only preaches the mercy of God for the sinner. He shows it in his own attitudes and actions.

(a) Read for yourselves Luke 7:36–50. Describe in your own words why the Pharisees criticised Jesus, and the meaning of Jesus's answer.
(b) Compare closely the account of the crucifixion in Luke 23:32–43 with Mk 15:22–39 and Matt. 27:33–50. Which *two* words of Jesus are given by Luke but not by Mark or Matthew? In what way are they relevant to the theme of Jesus and sinners?

## Women

In the Palestine of Jesus's day the sexes were far from being regarded as equal. Women were thought of as greatly inferior to men, and were discriminated against both socially and in religious matters. In view of this, Jesus's attitude to women is remarkable. Luke brings it out clearly in a number of ways.

(a) In the infancy narratives Luke gives to women a large part in God's plan of salvation: he writes of Elizabeth, of Anna, but above all of Mary, on whom much of the story is centred.

(b) He gives details (8:1–3) of the women who followed Jesus during his life of preaching. He tells the story of the sinful woman, and how Jesus defended her against the Pharisee (see above). He alone tells the story of Martha and Mary (10:38–42); and three times in his account of the passion he makes special mention of women (23:27–31; 23:49 and 55).

(c) Among the parables told only by Luke are two which are concerned especially with women. The Parable of the Lost Coin has already been mentioned. The other is the Parable of the Widow who made herself a nuisance (18:1–8), where even a bothersome woman is presented as an example of perseverance in prayer.

(d) Finally, among the miracle stories told only by Luke are two which are about women. One is the miracle of the physically-handicapped woman in 13:10–13. The other is that of the son of the widow of Naim. The latter has one remarkable detail. It is characteristic of Luke's gospel to be very restrained with regard to expressions of emotion. But he makes an exception in the case of the widow of Naim. Far from avoiding any reference to emotion, he emphasises the widow's loneliness (she was a *widow* and this was her *only* son), and in the face of the widow's grief Jesus is *moved by compassion*.

Above it was stated that it is characteristic of Luke's gospel to be very restrained with regard to expressions of emotion. Test this for yourselves by comparing the following couplets. Use columns to make your findings clear:

| Mark | Luke |
| --- | --- |
| 1:41 – compare | 5:13 |
| 1:43 – compare | 5:14 |
| 3: 5 – compare | 6:10 |
| 6:34 – compare | 9:11 |
| 10:14 – compare | 18:16 |
| 10:21 – compare | 18:22 |
| 14:33, 34 – compare | 22:40 |

# 18 The way of the Lord

At least one group of Christians today, the Society of Friends, uses a very simple expression for Christianity. They call it simply *The Way*. They have not invented this on their own: the use of this expression comes really from the gospel according to Luke.

The previous two chapters of this book have concentrated on the events, sayings, miracles and parables which are peculiar to Luke's gospel – those which are not told either by Mark or by Matthew. The previous chapter also noted certain small but deliberate verbal *changes*. But Luke has not only *inserted* and *changed*. He has also *omitted* certain sections of Mark (notably, the whole of 6:45–8:26 and 9:41–10:12) and the effect of these omissions is worth looking at.

In brief, what Luke has done is to miss out the sections in Mark which describe Jesus's journeys into Bethsaida, Tyre and Sidon, Decapolis and beyond the Jordan, and to replace them by a big chunk of Lucan material (9:51–18:14) describing what happened while Jesus was on his way to Jerusalem.

The effect of this is to divide the gospel of Luke (excluding the infancy narratives) into three sections. The first describes the ministry of Jesus in Galilee (4:14–9:50); the last, the ministry of Jesus in Jerusalem (19:28–21:38). And between the two, dominating the gospel in a sense, the journey of Jesus to Jerusalem.

The emphasis on the journey seems deliberate. The journey section begins: *As the days were drawing near when he was to be taken up, he set his face resolutely towards Jerusalem* (9:51). The reader is constantly reminded of Jesus's destination. The people (Samaritans) would not receive him because *his face was set towards Jerusalem* (9:53). Later (13:22), we are told that *he went on his way through towns and villages, teaching and journeying towards Jerusalem*. And the miracle of the ten lepers is set in this context: *On the way to Jerusalem* (17:11).

There are other allusions in the gospel which suggest that this was not merely a question of geography. For Luke, Jerusalem had special significance as the goal of Jesus's earthly life. Luke's gospel begins in *Jerusalem*, with Zechariah offering incense in the temple, and it ends with the disciples returning to *Jerusalem* (24:33) . . . and *continually in the temple* (24:53). In the infancy narratives (which summarise Luke's main themes) the child Jesus is twice taken *to Jerusalem* by his parents; and in the second of these incidents (which are told only by Luke) the temple in Jerusalem is his *Father's house* where Jesus must be (2:49). It is noteworthy too that in the account of the temptations, which Matthew and Luke probably drew from the same source, the order of the temptations is different (compare Matt. 4:1–11 and Luke 4:1–13). In Luke's account the placing of Jesus on the pinnacle of the temple is put last: what seemed a natural climax in Matthew (all the kingdoms of the world) is made subordinate by Luke to the importance of Jerusalem and the temple.

One other detail, shown by a comparison between Luke 9:28–36 (the Transfiguration) and its source in Mark 9:2–8. Mark just says that Moses and Elijah were talking to Jesus. Luke says that they talked about his *departure, which he was to accomplish at Jerusalem*. This addition which Luke makes has significance. The word here translated *departure* is the Greek word *exodos* (our 'exodus'), and this *exodus* is seen as something which Jesus will not just suffer, but *accomplish*. In other words, Jesus's *exodus* (with all the overtones of that word), his *passing-over* to the Father, which takes place *in Jerusalem*, is the climax of his life.

## The Way

So it is much more than a question of geography. Jesus does not just travel to Jerusalem: he *sets his face to go to Jerusalem*. It is his destiny as well as his destination. Only Luke gives us the message that Jesus sent to Herod (13:32): *Go and tell that fox: behold I cast out demons and perform cures today and tomorrow, and the third day I finish my course. Nevertheless I must go on my way today and tomorrow and the day following; for it cannot be that a prophet should perish away from Jerusalem*. The *exodus* he is to *accomplish* there is according to the plan of God; for *the Son of man goes as it is determined* (22:22). Mark's gospel, as we saw, is often described as a passion narrative with an introduction. Luke's gospel is also dominated by the passion, death and resurrection of Jesus, but in a different way. Through what seems at first merely a way of structuring his story, or simply a matter of geography, Luke is able to show Jesus's exodus, his pass-over, his death and resurrection, as the goal of his whole life.

### Following on the way

And it is the goal of his disciples too. When Mark wanted to express what is meant by being a disciple of Jesus, he talked about losing one's life to save it, about carrying one's cross. Luke talks above all about *following* Jesus.

Look up the references from Luke's gospel listed below. Can you detect a difference between the use of the verb *to follow* in the passages listed under A, and the way it is used in the passages under B?
A passages:    7:9;  9:11; 18:43; 22:10; 22:39; 22:54.
B passages:    5:11;  5:27;  5:28;  9:49;  9:57;  9:59;
                    9:61; 18:22; 18:28.
Summarise your conclusions.

Luke's use of the word in the sense of discipleship is strengthened by the many references, particularly in the section 9:51–19:27, to Jesus and his disciples going along the road, going on their way .... Although at one level this is a geographical reference, at another level it suggests that discipleship is seen above all as a following of Jesus, a walking in his way. This is confirmed if we turn to Luke's second book, the Acts of the Apostles. There it says that the witnesses to Jesus, those who saw him risen, were those who came up with him from Galilee to Jerusalem. Moreover, the Christian way of life, in the Acts, is simply described as the *way of salvation*, the *way of the Lord*, the *way of God*. And finally the Christian community itself, in this same book, is referred to simply as *the Way*. (If you are curious, look up Acts 13:30–33; 16:17; 18:25 and 26; 19:9; 19:23; 22:4; 24:14; 24:22.)

## The way of prayer

When it comes to specific instructions given by Jesus to those who follow him, Luke does not depart radically from Mark, though he allows himself a certain freedom (for example, he transposes Mk 6:7 – Jesus's instructions to the twelve – and applies them not only to the apostles in 9:1–6, but in a longer form to the seventy in 10:1–12). But one special emphasis characterises the gospel of Luke. His followers must be men of *prayer*. Luke has more teaching on prayer than either Mark or Matthew.

(a) Luke's gospel opens and closes with prayer: in the opening scene Zechariah is in the temple, and the people are *praying outside* (1:10); and at the end Luke shows the apostles, back in Jerusalem, *continually in the temple blessing God* (24:53).

(b) Those who prepare the way for Jesus, and are themselves open to his coming, are people of prayer. Zechariah is told that his *prayer is heard* (1:13). Anna worshipped in the temple night and day with *fasting and prayer* (2:38). And only Luke says that John the Baptist taught his disciples to pray (5:33 and 11:1).

(c) Jesus himself is shown frequently in prayer. He prays at his baptism (3:21); before choosing his twelve apostles (6:12); before Peter's confession of faith (9:18); before the transfiguration (9:28); before teaching the Lord's Prayer (11:1); on the Mount of Olives (22:42) and on the cross (23:46). When the fame of his miracles brought crowds round him, he *withdrew to the wilderness and prayed* (5:16). In 10:21–2 Luke gives the content of his prayer of thanksgiving. And Luke is the only evangelist who presents the Lord's Prayer as Jesus's direct answer to his followers who ask him to teach them to pray (11:2).

(d) Jesus specifically tells his disciples to pray (10:2). And in 11:9–13 Jesus speaks encouragement to those who pray.

(e) Among the parables peculiar to Luke are two which are about prayer: the Parable of the Importunate Friend (or the friend who made himself a nuisance: 11:5–8); and the Parable of the Judge and the Widow (18:1–6) (Look up both these parables. What is the point of each?)

## Led by the Spirit

In the Christian vocabulary, God as power of love at work in people's minds and hearts, giving them insight, joy and courage, is called the *Holy Spirit*. One great Christian of the first century, Paul, described the Christian way of life as *walking in the Spirit*. It is not surprising that Luke, who sees the following of Jesus as a walking in his way and a walking in prayer, is also the one who most frequently speaks of the action of the Holy Spirit.

There are seventeen or eighteen references to the Spirit in Luke's gospel, as compared with twelve in Matthew's and six in Mark's. More important than the number of references, however, is the part given by Luke to the Spirit in the story of Jesus and those who follow his way.

This is already greatly emphasised in the infancy narratives.

Read carefully the infancy narratives in Luke (that is, chapters 1 and 2), and note for yourselves all the references to the Holy Spirit. Then write a short essay showing how Luke sees the birth of Jesus, and the events surrounding it, as brought about by the working of God's Spirit in the world.

The infancy narratives, as was shown earlier, summarise the main themes of Luke's gospel. The idea that man's salvation is the work of the Holy Spirit is an idea Luke continues to bring out in the succeeding chapters.

The one who first proclaimed the good news of Jesus Christ, John the Baptist, said that Jesus would baptise people *with the Holy Spirit* (3:16). Jesus's own proclamation is 'steered', as it were, by the Spirit within him. At his baptism this is symbolised by the dove descending upon him (3:22). He is then *led by the Spirit* during his forty days in the desert (4:1), and after his temptation, says Luke, he *returned by the power of the Spirit into Galilee* (4:14). For his first public sermon he chose as his text (and applied it to himself) the passage from Isaiah which beings: The *Spirit of the Lord is upon me* . . . (4:18). The action of the Spirit is seen in him when he marvels at the ways of God his Father: *In that same hour he rejoiced in the Holy Spirit and said: I thank thee, Father, Lord of heaven and earth, that thou hast hidden these things from the wise and understanding, and revealed them to little ones* (10:21). The gift of the Spirit is the supreme gift of God to men (11:13) and resistance to the Spirit is the greatest evil (12:10). Jesus promises his followers that the Holy Spirit will be with them to guide them in their most difficult moments: *for the Holy Spirit will teach you in that hour what you ought to say* (12:12).

And his last command to his followers is to wait in Jerusalem for the coming of that Spirit: *Stay in the city until you are clothed with power from on high* (24:49). The fulfilment of that promise and the way in which faith in Christ was spread in the power of the Spirit, become the theme of Luke's second book, the Acts of the Apostles.

# 19 The good news for all time: the resurrection

Before beginning this chapter, read carefully Mk 16:1–20; Matt. 28:1–20; and Lk. 24:1–53. Analyse their contents in three parallel columns. Compare your results with the analysis on pp. 154 and 155.

| Mark | Matthew | Luke |
|---|---|---|
| (16:1–8) | (28:1–15) | (24:1–11) |
| The angel to the women | The angel to the women | The angel to the women |
| He is risen | He is not here | Why do you seek the living among the dead? |
| He is not here. | He is risen as he said. | |
| Tell the disciples and Peter he will meet you in Galilee. | He is going before you into Galilee. Jesus met them and said: Do not be afraid | |
| They said nothing | | They told the others who thought it *idle talk* and did not believe. |
| | (The guards' story: see also 27:62–66) | |

| Mark | Matthew | Luke |
|---|---|---|
| (16:9–11) | | |
| Jesus appears to Mary Magdalene. The disciples did not believe. | (Nothing in Matthew or Luke about this. The story is told more fully by John) | |

| Mark | | Luke |
|---|---|---|
| (16:12–13) | | (24:13–35) |
| Jesus appears *in another form* to two of them as they were walking into the country. | | A traveller joins two disciples going to Emmaus He said: Was it not necessary that the Christ should suffer? . . . Beginning with Moses . . . he interpreted . . . the things concerning himself. They recognised him . . . in the breaking of bread. |
| They told the others but they did not believe. | | They returned and told the others . . . who had heard of the resurrection from Peter. |

| (16:14) | | (24:36–49) |
|---|---|---|
| To the eleven at table | | To the apostles ... Why are you troubled? Shows hands and feet ... eats fish ... Opened their minds to understand scriptures. |

| (16:15–20) | (28:16–20) | (24:50–53) |
|---|---|---|
| | With the eleven on mountain | Led them out to Bethany |
| Go into the whole world | Go and teach all nations ... | preached to all nations ... you are witnesses. |
| He was taken up into heaven | | was carried up into heaven |
| They went forth and preached everywhere. | | They returned to Jerusalem with great joy. |

For Matthew, Mark and Luke the resurrection of Jesus is the reality behind the whole of the gospel story. It makes the good news. They understand the life and death of Jesus in a new light because of it. A Christian, who believes that God raised Jesus to a new life after death, sees his own life and his own death in a new light because of it. The resurrection of Jesus is what the Christian community stands for and stands by.

It is therefore rather surprising at first to see how briefly – even casually – at the end of the gospels the story of the resurrection is told. There is no attempt to write it up, give it headliness, make a sensation of it. The gospel writers do not even try to compose one story which hangs together in all its details. For example, Matthew locates the last farewell of Jesus to his disciples in Galilee (Matt. 28:16), whereas Luke sets it just outside Jerusalem (Lk. 24:50) and Mark does not give it any geographcial location at all (Mk 16:19). Such apparent contradictions do not seem to worry them at all. There is no attempt at argument or explanation. The basic message is simple: Jesus is alive – and they must preach this reality to the whole world.

Some people have tried to explain away the resurrection by suggesting:
(a) that Jesus did not really die at all; he went into some sort of a coma and recovered;
(b) that after Jesus had been buried, his disciples came during the night and took away his body, and then made up the story of the resurrection;
(c) that it was wishful thinking. The disciples were expecting him to rise from the dead as he had said he would, so they imagined it;

(cont'd)

(d)  that he was not really alive after his death. It was a ghost they saw.

   Careful reading of the gospel stories suggests that the gospel-writers had heard of these suggestions and took care to disprove them, not by arguing, but simply by details in the story they tell. Can you pick out the passages and show how they relate to one or other of these attempted explanations? (To help you: look particularly at Mk 15:42–6; Matt. 27:62–6; Mk 16:9–14; Lk. 24:13–23; Lk. 24:36–43).

   What do you think of these suggested explanations?

As for the gospel writers themselves, it is clear that they were convinced of the reality of the resurrection. The story which above all others helps the reader to see it as they saw it is Lk. 24:13–32, the story of the two disciples going to Emmaus. It gathers into itself and makes clearer much that other stories hint at or say more briefly.

### The Emmaus story (Lk. 24:13–35)

At the moment of the crucifixion, with the exception of some women who stood *at a distance* (Lk. 23:49), the disciples had *all left him* and fled. They did not even care about what happened to his body; it was left to a member of the Sanhedrin *who was looking for the kingdom of God* (Lk. 23:51) to see to his burial. In this context it is not surprising to find two of them walking away from Jerusalem. Their mood is one of sadness, despondency and disillusionment. *We had hoped* ... They meet a stranger, and tell him of the events of the last days, surprised indeed that he had not heard of them. They mention that it is the *third day*, but do not suggest in any way that they were expecting anything to happen. On the contrary, they know that the women have spread some story about his being alive, but that they cannot believe. For them the whole adventure is over.

   The stranger talks to them of the Scriptures. He draws upon the five books of Moses and also on the prophets to show them the kind of picture of the Messiah which comes out of their holy writings. He (the Messiah) was not to be a triumphant nationalistic leader (maybe that was what they had been expecting?) but one who would suffer and die, and *so enter into his glory*. As they listen, they understand (*he opened to us the scriptures*). Their mood changes, and they feel a response within themselves to what the stranger is saying, a response which they themselves describe later as *our hearts burning within us*. The stranger is nevertheless still a stranger, until they invite him to share a meal with them in the inn. At table he reproduces the action of Jesus at the Last Supper – and they recognise him. No sooner have they done so than he is there no longer. But they are changed. They go *that same hour* back to Jerusalem, and share their experience with the others, only to discover that the others have something to tell in their turn.

Suddenly Jesus is standing in their midst. In spite of all that they had just been saying, they think it is some sort of ghost, and are frightened. He reassures them that it is really he by showing them his hands and feet (presumably still marked by the wounds of the crucifixion) and by eating with them. And once again he shows from the scriptures the place of his death and resurrection in the plan of God.

The impression these stories give is of the evangelist struggling to express an experience so unusual, so unique, that it cannot be described except by statements which seem almost like riddles. Jesus is present and disappears, is flesh-and-blood yet cannot be held. Understanding his new way of being present is connected with understanding the whole history of God's relationship with men as told in the Scriptures. Everything is seen as leading up to this great event. This understanding grows out of a shared experience, yet no one in these stories believes just because he has been told. He or she has to have a personal moment of recognition, of seeing, when he is able to recognise what is not obvious to everybody. And in the Emmaus story this ability to recognise Jesus in a simple everyday experience is deliberately linked to the *breaking of bread*. We shall never know exactly what it was that convinced these first witnesses of the reality of Jesus's resurrection. But that they were convinced there is no doubt, and the gospels are written out of this conviction.

*Note* Christians today have the same kind of difficulty in describing the grounds of their own conviction. When pressed, they answer along similar lines: it is something to do with what is written in the gospels; something to do with the experience of Jesus's presence in their daily lives; something to do with an inner conviction (which they call faith); and something to do with their celebration of his resurrection in the *breaking of bread*, the Christian eucharist.

They picture it to themselves in different ways, according to how they understand the world in general. Some think of the resurrection above all as Jesus's spirit re-entering and giving life again to his body, so that the references to the empty tomb in the gospel are very important to them. Others think more of Jesus entering into a totally new kind of life, which enables him to be present in a new way to the world, and to lead men, through the influence of his spirit, to goodness, love, justice and peace. But all of them, like the gospel writers, would say that it cannot be proved, but has to be believed. Christianity stands by this belief.

Finally, in all three of the synoptic gospels, Jesus concludes his appearances to his followers by sending them to preach the good news which they have received. *Go into the whole world* (Mk 16:15) ... *make disciples of all nations* (Matt. 28:19) ... *repentance and the forgiveness of sins ... preached in his (Jesus's) name to all nations ... You are witnesses of these things* (Lk. 24:47)

Look up the passages from which the quotations on the previous page come, and compare the different accounts of Jesus's last appearance. What have they all in common?

## The gospel in the making

The second volume of Luke's work, which we call the Acts of the Apostles, tells us how the first followers of Jesus obeyed his command. They had few resources, neither money nor positions of influence, but their preaching carried conviction, and by the time the gospels came to be written there were Christian communities scattered throughout Asia Minor, Greece and Rome.

This book has maintained:

(a) that the gospels are part of this preaching, part of the self-expression of the early Church to which both the writers and their readers belonged;

(b) that they were written by individual writers, each with his own characteristics and personal viewpoint, for particular groups of Christians, with their varied cultural, social and political backgrounds;

(c) that they are marked by the situations in which and for which they were written, yet they are all part of the same proclamation, the same basic Christian experience. This is why they have remained vitally important to the whole Church throughout the centuries to this day.

(d) that they use basically the same method of proclaiming their message. The method was invented, as far as we know, by Mark. In one hand they hold the memories of Jesus, the carpenter of Nazareth, who walked the roads of Galilee preaching and doing good. In the other hand they hold their faith in Jesus raised by the Father to new life, and become for everyone the full expression of God's power and love (or as John's gospel was to put it later, the Word of God.) And they let go of neither. This is how they proclaim their faith in Jesus the Lord.

This book has tried to see the three evangelists at work, to catch the gospels in the making. There are other ways – other good ways – of reading the gospels. Some Christians feel such respect for these their most sacred and precious writings that they are reluctant to analyse them in this scientific kind of way. But behind the method used here is the confidence that careful and trustworthy scholarship can only help the reader to understand more fully their true nature, and therefore to hear more clearly what they have to say.

The gospels do not try to prove anything. Written by believers, mainly for believers, they assert, they proclaim, they say what is. Throughout the centuries they have enabled those who believe in Jesus Christ to know and love him better, and to live out his teaching, to follow the guidance of his Spirit, in their lives. Many who did not believe have been attracted by the person of Jesus as he is portrayed in the gospels, and by the goodness of his actions and his teaching. But the gospels do not force acceptance. They leave the reader free to accept or not the good news which they proclaim. Born out of the faith of the early Christian communities, what they say rings true to the experience of generations of believers. The gospels as documents were written by about the end of the first century. But a Christian would say that the gospel as Good News, the proclamation of Jesus the Christ, is in the making to the end of time.

Look back at the *Note* on p. 19. Re-read it carefully. What do you now think about the question it discussed?

# Questions for further work and revision

These questions are provided in order to help you to revise and to give you practice in organising your ideas and putting them down in writing. Some of them can be answered by referring to one particular chapter in the book; for others you will have to search more widely, using the index. Many of the questions (like others which you have already met in the course of this book) could provide an outline for a special assignment or course work, to be included as part of your final assessment.

1  (a) Where did Mark, Matthew and Luke get their material from? In other words, what were their sources?
(b) Where was each of these gospels probably written, and for what kind of Christian community?
(c) Give one example from each gospel to show how the emphasis of that particular gospel is related to the Christians for whom it was written.

2  (a) Describe one incident in Mark's gospel in which Jesus is shown as a man of authority.
(b) By referring to other incidents, show how Mark builds up this impression of Jesus as a person of authority.
(c) What do you think the word 'authority' means when Mark uses it of Jesus?

3  (a) What is meant by the 'Messianic secret' in Mark?
(b) Mention three miracles described in Mark in which Jesus tells people not to talk about what has happened, and one which is an exception to this rule.
(c) Re-read on p. 40 the various explanations of the 'Messianic secret' suggested by New Testament scholars. Explain the one which you think sounds the most likely. Give your reasons.

4  (a) What is meant by the word 'parable'? What is the difference between a parable and an allegory?
(b) Give one example from Mark's gospel, and another from Matthew's, in which a parable has been expanded into an allegory. Treat one of these in more detail, saying what you think was the original lesson of the parable as Jesus told it, and what it came to mean in the early Church.

5  (a) Tell the story of the Gerasene demoniac as told by Mark (5:1–20)
(b) Comment on three unusual features of this miracle.
(c) Why do you think Mark includes this story here? What is he

saying about Jesus? How is it related to the main theme of his gospel?

6 (a) With the help of the index, collect all that we can know from these three gospels about John the Baptist.

(b) Why does Luke give so much detail about John the Baptist's birth, and Mark so much detail about his death?

7 (a) Narrate the miracle of the Syro-Phoenician woman's daughter as told by Mark (7:24–30)

(b) What significance is there in the fact that she was a pagan, and that Jesus did what she asked?

(c) In what way could this miracle be described as a turning point in Jesus's ministry?

(d) How do (i) the healing of the deaf-and-dumb man and (ii) the feeding of the four thousand reinforce the point made by this miracle?

(e) What alterations does Matthew make to the sequence Mark 7:1–8:10 so as to make the point even more sharply?

8 *Who do men say that I am*? (a) Show how Mark, in the first eight chapters of his gospel, is constantly raising the question, directly or indirectly, of who Jesus is.

(b) Why is 8:27–30 important in this context?

9 (a) What kind of deliverer (= Messiah = Christ) were the Jews of Jesus's time expecting?

(b) What actions and words of Jesus does Mark record so as to change this expectation?

10 Jesus foretells his passion and death three times in Mark's gospel. From the setting of these 'foretellings' show how this gospel stresses the failure of his followers to grasp the meaning of his words.

11 Tell in your own words the parable of the Vineyard (Mark 12:1–12).

(b) What is its main point?

(c) On what other occasions, according to Mark 11–15, did Jesus challenge, by his words or by his actions, the Jewish authorities of his day?

12 (a) What do you know about the great religious festivals of the Jewish year?

(b) What references to any of them do you find in Mark 11–16?

13 (a) What is known about (i) the political and (ii) the legal situation of Palestine at the time of Jesus's death?

(b) What part is played in Jesus's trial and condemnation by (i) the Sanhedrin and (ii) Pilate?

14 Choose two miracle stories which are told by both Mark and Matthew.

(a) What alterations has Matthew made to Mark's account?

(b) Can you show that these alterations are related to Matthew's purpose in his gospel?

15 Many scholars think that Matthew wants to present Jesus as the New Moses. What evidence have we for this?

16 *Think not that I have come to abolish the law and the prophets. I have come not to abolish them but to fulfil them.*

(a) Can you show from Matthew 5–7 that this was true of the teaching of Jesus?

(b) Can you think of any incidents in any of the synoptic gospels when Jesus's words or behaviour seem to go against his people's laws or traditions? How did he justify himself in each case?

17 Drawing on all the synoptic gospels, show that Jesus preached forgiveness by word and deed.

18 Examine the instructions which Jesus, in Matthew's gospel, gives to the apostles and disciples. (Look particularly at chapters 10 and 18.)

(a) What qualities do you think Matthew would hope to find in the Church leaders of his day?

(b) Do you think the same qualities would be appropriate for bishops and other church leaders today?

19 What great truths concerning the person of Jesus do (a) Matthew and (b) Luke teach through the stories about his birth and childhood?

20 Show from the synoptic gospels what Jesus's attitude was to 'tax-collectors and sinners'. Which gospel emphasises this most strongly?

21 (a) Who were the Samaritans?

(b) Why did the Jews dislike them so much?

(c) What do we learn from the synoptic gospels about Jesus's own attitude to the Samaritans?

22 (a) Who were the following groups of people:

(b) (i) Pharisees (ii) Sadducees (iii) scribes (iv) Herodians? On what occasions did they come into conflict with Jesus? Explain the point of the conflict in each case.

23 What may be learned from (a) Matthew's gospel and (b) Luke's gospel about prayer in the life of a Christian?

24 Why is Luke's gospel sometimes called the *gospel of the Holy Spirit*?

25 In Mark 16: 9–20 we have a summary of the resurrection stories told more fully by Matthew and Luke. Read again the fuller accounts, and answer these questions:

(a) In which of these stories is Jesus not known at once, but there is a moment of recognition?

(b) What does this suggest to you?

(c) If all the stories resurrections except one were to be lost to the world, which one do you think Christians would want to keep above all? Make your own choice, and say why you think that particular story is so important.

Examination assessment has become much more concerned with the *skills* of understanding and evaluation and less with a body of content-based *knowledge*. The style of questions now set in examinations is designed to meet these new criteria. Assignments, in particular, will be assessed with special reference to the objectives of understanding and evaluation. The following grid shows how the above questions are related to the assessment objectives specified by the National Criteria for Religious Studies.

| Question | Knowledge | Understanding | Evaluation |
|---|---|---|---|
| 1 | (a)  (b) | (b)  (c) | (c) |
| 2 | (a)  (b) | (b) | (c) |
| 3 | (b) | (a) | (c) |
| 4 | (b) | (a)  (b) | |
| 5 | (a) | (b) | (c) |
| 6 | (a) | (b) | |
| 7 | (a) | (b)  (c)  (e) | (d) |
| 8 | | (a) | (b) |
| 9 | (a) | (b) | |
| 10 | | Whole question | |
| 11 | (a) | (b)  (c) | |
| 12 | (a) | (b) | |
| 13 | (b) | (a) | |
| 14 | | (a) | (b) |
| 15 | | | Whole question |
| 16 | (a) | (b) | (b) |
| 17 | | Whole question | |
| 18 | | (a) | (b) |
| 19 | | | (a)  (b) |
| 20 | | Whole question | |
| 21 | (a)  (c) | (b)  (c) | |
| 22 | (a) | (b) | (b) |
| 23 | | Whole question | |
| 24 | | Whole question | Whole question |
| 25 | (a) | | (b)  (c) |

# Index